A PHOTOGRAPHIC GUIDE TO

TRACKS
AND
TRACKING
IN SOUTHERN AFRICA

LOUIS LIEBENBERG

CONTENTS

INTRODUCTION: THE ART OF TRACKING

Tracking may well be among the oldest of the sciences. It is also one of the most revealing: trackers gain a detailed understanding of animal behaviour through the interpretation of their tracks and signs, accumulating information – especially on seldom-seen rare or nocturnal species – which might otherwise remain unknown.

Moreover, tracks and signs illuminate natural behaviour, while direct observation often influences the animal by the mere presence of the observer. Tracking is thus a less invasive process than visual study, a method of information gathering in which the amount of stress inflicted on an animal is minimized.

One of the most important aids to successful nature conservation is, undoubtedly, an awareness of wildlife among the general public. Even keen nature lovers are often oblivious to the wealth of animal life around them, simply because most animals are rarely seen. Indeed, ignorance may well be the single most dangerous threat to species survival posed by human 'progress'. The ability to recognize living forms from the signs they leave helps create that awareness.

SIL/CLB

An African landscape: seemingly empty, but rich in wildlife

To the untrained eye the wilderness can appear desolate, but to someone who is 'spoor conscious' it will be full of life. Even if you never actually catch sight of the animals, you know that they are there, and by reconstructing their movements from the signs they leave behind, you will be able to visualize them, 'see' them in your mind's eye. In this way a whole story will unfold – a story of what happened when no-one was looking.

Using this book

The species accounts in these pages are arranged in logical order, from reptiles and amphibians through the ground-feeding birds to the mammalian predators and herbivores. Each account carries at least one full-colour photograph of the relevant life form, illustrations of the footprint and, where appropriate, of other signs, and a brief description of the animal, its size, habitat, habits, food, spoor and other signs of its presence. The measurements given are those which the author has personally recorded. In some instances, additional research is needed before the correct median – the average – can be firmly established.

The overall coverage is selective rather than comprehensive: we have included the more common birds and reptiles (snakes appear in a composite entry) and most, though not all, the mammals. Of special interest is the feature (pages 14 and 15) on the tracks and signs of some of the more common insects one finds in veld and garden, and, on pages 136 and 137, a 'gallery' of pictures comprising a representative selection of animal droppings. Distribution maps have been included where appropriate. Also included are a detailed Content's list, Glossary and Index.

Tracks and signs

Tracking involves each and every indication of an animal's presence, including ground spoor, vegetation spoor, scent, feeding signs, urine, faeces, saliva, pellets, territorial signs, paths and shelters, vocal and other auditory signs, visual signs, incidental signs, circumstantial signs and skeletal signs.

Footprints provide the most detailed information on the identity, movements and activities of animals in the wild. The spoor illustrations in this book derive from precise studies made under ideal conditions.

In reality, though, one seldom finds two animals of the same species with identical footprints: nature simply does not work in that way. But these 'ideal' footprints do provide images that improve one's chances of recognizing spoor that may otherwise be overlooked. Conversely, the preconceived images could prompt 'recognition' of patterns in markings made by other animals, or even random markings, so one must be careful not see simply what one wants to see.

While species may be recognized by general characteristics, each individual animal's spoor has its subtle distinctions, differences dictated by age, mass, sex, physical condition, the local terrain and the wider region (the nature of which gives rise to functional and environmental adaptations). The animal may also have a unique way of walking or a particular habit that distinguishes it from others. And, of course, there are random variations.

Thus, for example, the Bushman trackers of the Kalahari, whose skill has been honed over the many generations, can follow a particular antelope, perhaps one they have wounded, and distinguish it from the rest of the herd. They are also able to track fellow humans, identifying not only the gender but the particular individual they are tracking. Women usually have smaller and narrower, and sometimes more 'curvaceous' feet than men; a slender body build usually means slender feet; stocky people tend to have shorter and broader feet. A person's spoor is characterized by the way he or she treads and walks, by the length of stride, the way the ball of the foot is twisted, the way the toes point and whether they are splayed or curled in, by the way the foot throws up small sprays of sand, and by the scuff marks. Each person covers the ground in unique fashion.

Louis Liebenberg

The Bushmen are master trackers; this is !Nate of Lone Tree, Botswana

Many animals in the wild are not so individualized. While the spoor of most of the larger mammals and birds will reveal the particular species to which they belong, those of the smaller animals may indicate only the broader genus, family or order. The smaller the animal, in short, the more difficult it becomes to pinpoint its precise classification.

The clearest footprints tend to be left in damp, slightly muddy earth, in wet sand, in a thin layer of loose dust on firm substrate (a dirt road or path, for example), and in snow. Usually, however, footprints are partially obliterated, and one should explore the area – walk up and down the trail – to find the best imprints. Even if no clear prints are discerned, the information from a number of footprints can be pieced together to produce a composite image of the complete spoor.

Soft sand is always a difficult spoor medium. Try to visualize the shape of the footprint before the loose grains rolled together to blur the edges. Bear in mind, too, that slipping and twisting will distort footprints in any kind of terrain: when the animal runs, or walks on a slope, its feet may slide and spoor will appear elongated or warped. Moreover, when the animal trots or runs, its mass is supported largely by the toes and only part of the intermediate pads may show (in the case of mongooses, the proximal pads may not show at all). Similarly, hard ground may only reveal claw marks.

When confronted by a choice of several possible species, consult the distribution maps in this book, eliminating those that do not occur in the area. Then narrow the list down by noting any feeding signs, faeces, and such elements of habit and habitat as daily rhythm and sociability.

Spoor identification requires field skill as well as knowledge. Although the novice naturalist should be able to use this book to identify near-perfect spoor in ideal conditions, it is only by accumulating experience that one learns to interpret imperfect signs, especially those imprinted in loose sand. Practice, as always, is the key to success.

Learning to track

Those who are not traditional hunters cannot really expect to reach the same level of skill as folk for whom tracking becomes part of their way of life in childhood, and whose very survival depends on their tracking abilities. This book, however, will introduce readers to the basics, help them identify species from the signs the animals leave behind. The average person should, with regular practice, be able to become a fair tracker. Among the qualities required are good eyesight (or good glasses), acute observation, a degree of physical fitness, patience, perseverance, concentration, imagination and a good memory.

The ease or difficulty of tracking at any given time also depends on a number of other factors. The type of ground and vegetation and weather conditions will determine the degree of skill needed to recognize and interpret spoor. It is more difficult, for example, to track in hard, stony terrain than in firm sand. Spoor lacks depth in overcast weather, while it may be obliterated entirely by rain. In areas of high animal densities the spoor may be blurred or otherwise confused.

The easiest way to learn the art of tracking is to have an experienced tracker teach you, to point out and explain all the signs until you are able to recognize and interpret them yourself. Bear in mind, though, that expert trackers are few and far between and many are unfamiliar with the English language.

A valid option is to teach yourself. This approach is much more time-consuming, of course, but it has its rewards, most notably the excitement and the sense of achievement that comes with making one's own discoveries.

Start by studying your own tracks. Adopt an initial two-phase approach, repeating the phases until they come together to become one sequence, as follows.

Phase One. Mark the starting point, and then lay out a spoor for yourself. Go back to the start, and study every sign of your passage. When you complete the course – which may take some while – return to the starting point.

Phase Two. The course now consists of two trails, and since you've been over it twice, you should know where it is going. This second phase involves simply walking over a familiar course at fast pace. Look well ahead of you, try to pick up as many signs in the wider area as possible. The objective is to develop the ability to anticipate and predict the unfamiliar.

In Phase One you focus on recognition and interpretation and ignore such aspects as momentum and anticipation. By Phase Two you are familiar with the spoor and should now concentrate on these aspects. You'll probably miss most of the signs on the first Phase Two run, but will recognize more of them, and more quickly, after going over the ground several times. The combined exercise should be repeated over different types of terrain, starting with an easy route, perhaps over softish sand, and gradually working up towards the more difficult types.

When you have developed an ability to track your own trail, get someone else to lay one down for you. This spoor will of course be more difficult. Obviously it is easier if you use a person rather than an animal as your quarry at this stage, since you can identify with another human being, and anticipate their movements by putting yourself in their position.

Phases One and Two involved the location and observation of each and every sign. In the third exercise, try to follow the trail by looking at only a few signs. Survey the terrain; try to imagine the most likely route the person would have taken; try to spot signs well ahead, neglecting those in between. Short cuts will save a lot of time and trouble. Indeed, if you know the area and the person well and can calculate his route through a certain point, skip the intermediate signs, go straight to that point and track the trail from there. If you lose the spoor, search other possible routes for signs. Should this prove unsuccessful, walk in a series of ever-widening circles in order to find fresh leads.

So much for the human trail: tracking wildlife poses much more of a challenge. Here, the best way to start is to watch the animal and, once it has moved off, approach and study its tracks.

Louis Liebenberg

Louis Liebenberg

Turtle track on sand   Red lechwe track on firm substrate

Follow the trail (you'll know the direction in which it moved); study the signs carefully so that you become familiar with its habits, its footprints, its gait. Gradually upgrade the challenge. Begin with easy terrain, such as the sand of beach dunes or that of an arid region, progressing to terrain with soft substrate and sparse vegetation, then to soft substrate and denser vegetation, then to harder, stony ground with sparser cover and finally to harder, stony substrate with dense vegetation. Eventually, as you build up experience, it will be possible to track an animal without observing all the signs: a skilled tracker will know the animal well enough to predict its movements.

Expert trackers will also need to know whether a spoor is fresh enough to follow up, or just too old to be worthwhile. Tracks of other animals that superimpose or underlie the spoor may help them to estimate its age. They will also have to tell when the spoor is so fresh, and the animal so close, that it will be alarmed if they do not approach it with stealth. Again, this requires knowledge of animal behaviour, a familiarity with local weather conditions, and a great deal of practice. The rate at, and the way in which the sun, wind and rain erode the tracks can vary considerably.

Study the aging process systematically. Lay out a series of spoor – say, one footprint each hour – over a full day. By evening you will have examples of spoor of varying ages, they can be compared directly, and you will be able to study the aging process at your leisure and in detail. Repeat the exercise in different kinds of soil, on different types of terrain, in different seasons and in various weather conditions.

Tracking in nature conservation

Trackers play a key role in the growing ecotourism industry, serving as the eyes and ears of those who embark on game-viewing drives and wilderness trails.

They are also crucial in anti-poaching operations. Intruders may be detected even when they leave no clearly discernible human footprints. For example, fleeing animals will leave tracks that indicate a disturbance – a human-inspired one if there are no signs of a natural predator. Scavenger spoor converging on a point may also indicate the presence of a large carcass, perhaps of an animal killed by poachers.

Louis Liebenberg

Karel Benadie with the
CyberTracker in the Karoo

Louis Liebenberg

Close-up of a CyberTracker: data
at the touch of a button

Expert trackers, able to garner information denied to conventional observers, also render valuable assistance to researchers studying animal behaviour. Combining traditional tracking with modern technology, such as radio tracking, allows the researcher to accomplish much more than either method could on its own.

At the leading edge of the technology is the CyberTracker field computer, a device that enables trackers to record all their field observations, and to store them in a database for future reference. An integrated Global Positioning System (GPS) records the location, time and date of each entry by means of satellite navigation. The data collected can also be fed into a Geographic Information System. All of which sounds rather complex, but in fact the system is easy to use in terms of both input and access: managers and other interested parties are able to call up the maps, tables and other graphics, to analyze data and to monitor long-term trends at the touch of a button.

READING THE SIGNS

Short of direct visual observation, an animal's track – its footprint – provides the surest clue to its presence (or passage) and its identity. However animals can often be detected and sometimes identified by a variety of other signs, including scuff marks, broken twigs, freshly turned stones, leaves and other objects, trampled and horned vegetation, river-bank mud displacement, droppings, pellets and latrines.

Droppings

Faeces are among the more obvious of these supplementary signs. Those of elephants, rhinos and hippos, for example, are large and rounded; hippos tend to scatter theirs with a paddle-like action of their tails, often found on or near the paths along the riverbanks that serve as their night-time feeding grounds. Rhinos defecate in territorial middens. Zebra dung has a distinctive and regular kidney shape; warthog droppings are similar in appearance, but more irregular and rounder.

Louis Liebenberg

Springhare droppings: almost rectangular with one pointed end

Antelope tend to have similar-shaped droppings – pellet-like, with a point at one end and an indentation at the other – so it can be hard to identify a particular species from this sign alone. Often, the best one can do is make a rough estimate of the animal's size (small, medium, large). Giraffe droppings are similar to the antelopes' but are larger and, because they fall from a height, tend to be scattered.

Most mammalian carnivores leave narrow, cylindrical or sausage-shaped droppings that are pointed at one end. Omnivores, such as baboons and honey badgers, also tend to produce cylindrical droppings, as do the plant-eating porcupines.

Droppings often reveal what an animal eats, which is a more than useful pointer to species identification. The dung of the black (hook-lipped) rhino, for example, contains the remains of twigs and leaves; the white (square-lipped) rhino's faeces reveal its grass diet. Carnivore faeces tend to show bone and hair; hyaenas, and sometimes lions, produce droppings that are whitish from the high calcium content of their bone diet. Conversely, a lion's faeces can often be black from the amount of blood it has consumed. Civet droppings are invariably characterized by a mixture of millipede shells, fruit pips, insect husks and fur and bone from the tiny mammals they prey on; those of otters and water mongooses by crabshells; aardvarks and aardwolfs by a mix of sand and termite remains; pangolins by sand and ant remains. Wetlands trees are frequently stained white with the guano of roosting herons, egrets and cormorants; white-stained rocks can indicate the nesting site of a Cape vulture, bald ibis, marabou stork, black eagle or some other raptor. Dassies stain the rocky outcrops among which they live white and dark brown with their urine.

Territorial markings

Many animals use their faeces to mark out their territories, and you'll often come across their waste, in huge quantities, in areas called middens or latrines. The animal keeps returning to its latrine, and in doing so leaves other signs of its presence, such as scrapings and rubbing posts. The latter are smooth, well-worn rocks, trees, or stumps used for scraping off dead skin, parasites and other unwanted matter.

Other territorial markings include clawing posts, ground that has been pawed, shrubbery horned, and twigs covered in tarry secretions produced by antelope – such as dik-dik, red duiker and blue duiker – in the preorbital gland. Vegetation is covered by secretions from the anal gland in hyaenas, polecats, civets and others. Some mammals – rhino, lion and leopard for instance – spray vegetation with their urine.

Feeding signs

Uprooted trees, scattered grass tufts, stripped bark and broken branches may indicate the presence of elephants, though by no means always: porcupines ringbark trees, as do many other rodents. Browsers leave jagged leaf-edges; the black rhino a neat, angular bite-mark on twigs. Other browsers deposit saliva – copious amounts of it, dripping down in streams in the case of the giraffe, which eats the leaves and flowers of thorny acacias.

The general nature of cropped vegetation is usually a good pointer to the type of animal that has been browsing. One can at least make a rough estimate of its size from the level at which it eats. Grazers also feed at different levels, and on different lengths of grass: buffalo and zebra prefer the longer type, around which they can wrap their tongues, while wildebeest and white rhino tend to crop close to the ground.

Among other useful feeding signs are carcasses and skeletons, which indicate recent activity and will convey some idea of the type of carnivore or scavenger that has been feeding. Generally

Carcasses provide good pointers to what killed the animals

Peter Pickford/SIL

speaking, the larger the carcass, the larger the predator. Beak and bite marks, and the part of the animal consumed, are significant pointers; so too is the position of the carcass: leopards, for instance, often carry their prey into a tree. Old rodent and other bones strewn beneath a tree will invariably pinpoint the location of a raptor's nest.

Birds, snakes and, often, hyaenas, regurgitate pellets of hair, shell, insect chitin, bones and other indigestible material. But look closely: the pellets can be confused with long, cylindrical dung, especially that of carnivores.

Other Signs

Nests, depressions in vegetation and holes in trees or the ground also serve as useful aids to identification. Squirrel tracks, for instance, almost always lead to and from a tree; keeping vigil over a tree hollow might well yield a sighting of squirrel, bushbaby or bird. Even more distinctive are birds' nests. The hamerkop's huge, dome-like structure is unmistakable; white-backed vultures make their acacia-based homes in untidy clusters of twigs; buffalo weavers construct untidy stick-nests, a little way down from the top of particular trees; swallows and swifts build mud nests on buildings and cliff-sides. Among the most eye-catching of all are the vast colonial nests fashioned by sociable weavers.

Then there's the all-purpose antbear (or aardvark) hole, originally excavated by this nocturnal insectivore and then given over to a whole succession of squatters. Many different species, including hyaena, warthog and mongoose, are known to use the antbear's abandoned home. The tracks and droppings around the hole, and indeed its size, will give one a good idea of which particular animal is in residence.

Wildlife in Miniature

Most terrestrial life forms leave signs of their presence in and passage through their home range – not least of all the arthropods, big and small, which inhabit our gardens and the countryside beyond. The tracks illustrated here (and best observed on smooth, sandy soil) are those of a few of our more familiar arthropods.

Caterpillar (picture by Leonard Hoffman/SIL)

Millipede (picture by Lex Hes)

Dung beetle (picture by Peter Pickford/SIL)

Termite (picture by Leonard Hoffman/SIL)

Grasshopper (picture by Leonard Hoffman/SIL)

Tenebrionid beetle (picture by Leonard Hoffman/SIL)

Scorpion (picture by Leonard Hoffman/SIL)

Frogs and Toads

A brightly coloured painted reed frog

Southern Africa is home to many species of these amphibians, collectively known as Anura. They are, of course, excellent swimmers and, on land, adapted for a leaping mode of loco- motion. **Size:** This ranges from the 18-mm microfrog to bullfrogs that grow to more than 200 mm in length. **Habitat:** Some frogs and toads are wholly aquatic; others semi-aquatic, inhabiting marshy ground near watercourses, vleis and dams. In general, toads prefer more open country and are generally less aquatic than frogs. **Habits:** Most species are active at night, and at twilight and just before dawn. **Food:** Insects, insect larvae and snails. **Spoor:** Anura have four toes on each forefoot and five toes on each hind foot. The hopping spoor of a toad shows the five toes of the hind feet and the imprints of the four toes of the forefeet. Other signs: The droppings, especially those of toads, are short and compact and contain the remains of insect exoskeletons and snail shells.

hind foot   hind foot

forefoot   forefoot

16

Land Tortoises · *Family Testudinidae*

These shell-backed and toothless reptiles are well represented in southern Africa. They are characterized by their dome-like shells and clawed feet. The region is home to 12 species. **Size:** Ranges from leopard tortoises (45 cm) to the speckled padloper (9 cm), the

Angulate tortoise

world's smallest. **Habitat:** Tortoises cannot tolerate temperature extremes, and need good ground cover in which to shelter from both heat and cold. **Habits:** For protection, the tortoise withdraws its head and limbs into its shell. Adult males are aggressive towards each other in the mating season. In very cold periods, tortoises find a sheltered place in which to hibernate. Tortoises lay eggs, which they bury in the ground to incubate. **Food:** Mainly plant matter, though some species eat snails, millipedes and other invertebrates; others will gnaw bones and even eat carnivore droppings for the calcium. **Spoor:** Two species, the greater padloper *Homopus femoralis* and the parrot-beaked tortoise *H. aerolatus*, have four claws on the fore- and hind feet. All other land tortoises, including three species of padlopers, have five claws on the forefeet and four on the hind feet. Claws may be dragged through soft sand; only the claw marks may show on hard ground. Other signs: Droppings, comprising mainly vegetable matter, resemble those of a small carnivore (cylindrical, and pointed at one end).

forefoot

hind foot

Side-necked Terrapins   *Family Pelomedusidae*

Anton Pauw

Louis Liebenberg

Terrapins occur in fresh water and are characterized by their webbed toes. There are two distinct types within the region: the common helmeted terrapin; and the hinged terrapins, of which there are five species. **Size:** 15–45 cm in length. **Habitat:** The helmeted terrapin is widespread, found wherever there are pans, lakes, rivers and swamps. They will also bask on logs, rocks and river banks. The hinged terrapins are confined to the northern areas. **Habits:** Like tortoises, terrapins retreat into their shells for protection but do so by bending their necks sideways. **Food:** Terrapins are carnivorous for the most part, feeding on fish, and on birds that come to the water to drink. They have also been known to scavenge at hippo, crocodile and antelope carcasses, and to feed on hippo skin, which they nip off (very painfully) near the anal area. **Spoor:** These terrapins have five claws on both the fore- and hind feet.

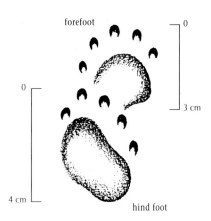

forefoot

0

0

3 cm

0

4 cm

hind foot

Sea Turtles   *Superfamily Chelonioidea*

Loggerhead turtle, Maputaland

Five species of these marine reptiles occur along southern Africa's coasts though only two, the giant leatherback and loggerhead, venture ashore. Limbs have been modified into flippers, which retain just one or two claws. Unlike tortoises and terrapins, the turtle cannot withdraw into its shell (or carapace). **Size:** 70–178 cm in length. **Habitat:** Leatherbacks and loggerheads arrive at their breeding grounds off southern Africa's eastern seaboard, from about Cape Vidal northwards, each year between November and January. **Habits:** Mating takes place offshore, the females crawling up the beaches at night to lay and bury their eggs. **Food:** Seaweed, seagrasses, jellyfish, combjellies, corals, sea urchins, giant clams, crustaceans (mostly shrimps, prawns and crabs) and fish. Not all turtles, however, are carnivorous; some species are restricted in their diet to seaweeds and seagrasses. **Spoor:** Loggerheads and leatherbacks leave a distinct trail on the beach sand.

Loggerhead turtle eggs.

Turtle tracks on beach.

Snakes   *Suborder Serpentes*

A young boomslang

These limbless, scaly reptiles vary widely in size, colour and markings. **Size:** From small up to 7 m in length. **Habitat:** Depends on the species, of which about 130 occur in southern Africa. Snakes are found in deserts and semi-arid areas, in forests, grasslands and even in the sea. All are cold-blooded, and are at their most active within their preferred temperature range of 20–32° Celsius. **Habits:** When ambient temperature becomes too hot snakes move into shade; in cold conditions they become sluggish; in very cold ones they may hibernate. They are highly sensitive to vibrations; vision is acute at short range, poor at a distance. **Food:** Most snakes prefer live prey (small mammals, birds, other reptiles, amphibians, insects and other invertebrates), which is swallowed whole.

Puff adder trail

Sand snake trail

Spoor: Snakes use their bodies to move in either rectilinear (caterpillar-like) or undulatory fashion.

Rectilinear progression – forward movement in a straight line – is characteristic of heavy-bodied snakes such as pythons and adders in leisurely mode. Here, the belly muscles move the large ventral plates (belly scales) forward in alternate waves to enable the overlapping plate-edges to get a grip on any roughness of the ground so that the body is drawn forward over them. With puff adders, there is usually a thin furrow down the middle of the trail where the snake has dragged the tip of its tail, and the ventral scales may leave clear markings. The spoor of puff adders and pythons can be distinguished by their ventral scales: the middle row of the puff adder's are almost as wide as the spoor itself; the python's is much narrower, so adjacent rows of scales also mark the spoor.

Undulatory or *serpentine progression* involves series of sideways motions, 'rippling' from front to back, where each outward bend or curve of the snake's body pushes up against an uneven or rough surface and propels the snake forward. Most snakes cover the ground in this way – including pythons and puff adders when they are in a hurry (it is much faster). The sidewinding variation, in which the body is lifted from the ground in undulating motions, is characteristic of small, desert-living adders (see cover photograph).

Other signs: Snakes moult periodically, and discarded skin may be found near their burrows.

The best time to follow snake spoor is in the early morning, before the wind obliterates the traces. To determine direction, study the way the sand or earth has been pushed back.

1. Typical snake 2. Puff adder (rectilinear) 3. Puff adder (undulatory)
4. Python (rectilinear) 5. Python (undulatory)

Rock Monitor   *Varanus albigularis*

Anton Pauw

A very large, stout lizard with strong, stocky limbs and sharp claws. The back is dark grey-brown with pale yellow, dark-edged blotches; limbs are spotted with pale yellow; the tail is banded in dark brown and off-white. **Size:** 70–110 cm in length. **Habitat:** Savanna and arid, karroid areas. **Habits:** Usually solitary; takes shelter in trees, often under loose bark. **Food:** Mainly invertebrates (millipedes, beetles, grasshoppers and land snails). Also scavenges on carrion. **Spoor:** Monitors have five toes on each fore- and hind foot; each toe has a strong, sharp claw. In muddy terrain, the scales underneath the toes show clearly in the spoor. The tail also leaves a clear drag mark.

forefoot
0
6 cm
0
11 cm
hind foot

Louis Liebenberg

22

Water Monitor

Varanus niloticus

Lex Hes

This reptile, the largest of the African lizards, has a stout body, powerful limbs and strong claws. It is greyish brown to dirty olive-brown on the top of its head and back, with scattered darker blotches and light yellow ocelli and bands on the head, back and limbs. Belly and throat are paler, with black bars. **Size:** 1–1.4 m in length. **Habitat:** Rivers, pans and major lakes; always found in the vicinity of permanent water. **Habits:** An excellent swimmer. **Food:** Forages in freshwater pools for crabs and mussels, frogs, fish, birds and their eggs. **Spoor:** Like that of the rock monitor (see opposite), this species' spoor shows five toes on the fore- and hind feet. The tail leaves a clear drag mark.

forefoot

0

6 cm

0

11 cm

hind foot

Louis Liebenberg

23

Nile Crocodile   *Crocodylus niloticus*

Shaen Adey/SIL

The largest of Africa's reptiles, occasionally reaching a mass of more than 1 000 kg. The nostril, eye and ear openings are located at the top of the head, projecting just above the surface when the animal is floating. **Size:** 2.5–3.5 m in length; max. 5.9 m. **Habitat:** Large rivers, lakes and swamps; river mouths, estuaries and mangrove swamps. **Habits:** Amphibious and riparian (river environment). Spends much of the day basking in the sun, on sand- or mudbanks, in order to gain heat; the rest of the time it remains semi-submerged. **Food:** Subadults feed on fish, insects, frogs, terrapins, birds and small mammals; adults mainly on fish, and on mammals as substantial as medium to large antelope, zebra and even buffalo, which are ambushed when they come to the water to drink. **Spoor:** Crocodiles have five toes on the forefeet and four on the hind feet. Each toe has a thick claw. The hind feet are webbed. In mud, the scales underneath the feet leave clear impressions in the spoor. The drag mark of the tail shows in the trail. The tracks of a young crocodile can be distinguished from that of monitors by the four hind toes (monitors have five). Other signs: These include the croaks of the young crocodiles while hatching and when they are in the nursery area. The remains of the large, white eggs, usually left on sandy patches, show where a crocodile has been breeding.

24

forefoot

0

11 cm

hind foot

0

25 cm

Roger de la Harpe/SIL

Nest of crocodile eggs

Louis Liebenberg

Passerines

Order Passeriformes

0

3.2 cm

Cape sparrow

Nigel Dennis/SIL

The order is represented by more than 5 000 small to large species worldwide, among them crows, ravens, sparrows, waxbills, canaries, buntings, wagtails, starlings, bulbuls, thrushes, chats and larks. They are represented in southern Africa by 29 families, most of which (about 80 per cent) are arboreal. Size, habits and feeding patterns vary widely. **Spoor:** Three toes in front, one behind, adapted for perching. No species has webbed toes. Passerine spoor will often superimpose or underlie, and therefore help to age, larger animal tracks.

Crows and Ravens

Family Corvidae

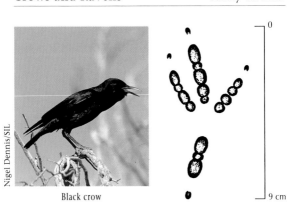

0

9 cm

Black crow

Nigel Dennis/SIL

Large, predominantly black birds with slender bills and large, strong feet. **Size:** 43–54 cm. **Habitat:** Wide tolerance. **Habits:** Usually seen in pairs, sometimes in flocks. These birds forage on the ground, walking with long strides. **Food:** Omnivorous. **Spoor:** Three forward-pointing toes, one pointing back at an angle.

Hornbills   *Family Bucerotidae*

0

6 cm

Jéan du Plessis

Yellowbilled hornbill

In southern Africa these would include the redbilled, yellowbilled and grey hornbills, all medium-sized birds with large, heavy, deeply curved bills, and the distinctive ground hornbill, which is treated separately (see page 28). Most are black, grey and white in colour with broad wings and long tails. **Size:** 42–60 cm. **Habitat:** Mainly forest, woodland and bushveld. **Habits:** Found singly, in pairs or small groups, foraging mostly on the ground but also in trees. **Food:** Insects. **Spoor:** Legs are very short (unlike those of the ground hornbill) and stout. Toes short, the third and fourth joined at the base; the claws short, curved and with sharp edges. All have similar spoor, with three forward-pointing toes and one backward-pointing toe.

Ground Hornbill

Bucorvus leadbeateri

Nigel Dennis/SIL

Louis Liebenberg

A very large turkey-like bird, mostly black with distinctive red wattles. **Size:** 90–129 cm. **Habitat:** Woodland, savanna, open grassveld, agricultural land. **Habits:** Forages on the ground; found in pairs or groups of, usually, not more than eight. **Food:** The ground hornbill is wholly carnivorous, its diet including reptiles, frogs, snails and insects. **Spoor:** Legs are long, toes short, the third and fourth joined at the base. Claws are short, curved and with sharp edges.

0

15 cm

Doves and Pigeons   *Family Columbidae*

Cape turtle dove

Medium-sized birds with short bills. **Size:** 19–36 cm. **Habitat:** Found everywhere – in woodland, forest, savanna, grassland, riverine bush, farmland, urban and rural gardens and city parks. **Habits:** Solitary or found in pairs or flocks. **Food:** Seeds, insects, fallen grain, winged termites, fruit. **Spoor:** These birds forage on the ground, walking with small steps in 'pigeon-toed' fashion to leave a winding trail. The different species have similar tracks, comprising three forward-pointing toes and a angled backward pointing toe. Dove footprints are smaller than those of pigeons. The Namaqua dove, smallest of the region's doves, has a dragging spoor.

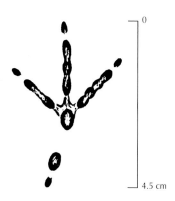

Crowned Plover

Vanellus coronatus

A fairly large plover with long, red legs. The face, chest and upper parts are greyish brown, the crown is black, ringed with white. A dark breastband separates the brown chest from a white belly. **Size:** 30 cm. **Habitat:** Short, dry grassland, burnt veld, lightly wooded savanna, semidesert. **Habits:** Gregarious, often active and vocal at night. **Food:** Insects. **Spoor:** Tracks show three forward-pointing toes (no back toe).

Spotted (Cape) Dikkop

Burhinus capensis

A medium-sized bird, spotted dark-brown or buff above, white below, with large, yellow eyes, and yellow legs and feet. **Size:** 42–44 cm. **Habitat:** Open grassland near trees or bushes, savanna, stony semidesert with scrub, wide marine beaches; also agricultural land. **Habits:** Found singly or in pairs; nocturnal and crepuscular. **Food:** Insects, crustaceans, molluscs, frogs, grass seeds. **Spoor:** The toes are short, and slightly webbed at the base. The hind toe is absent.

Coursers   *Family Glareolidae*

Doublebanded courser

Medium-sized birds with long legs. They are at their most active at night; the eyes are large. Cryptically coloured for camouflage in sandy or stony environment. **Size:** 20–28 cm. **Habitat:** Woodland with scrub layer, acacia savanna. **Habits:** Mainly nocturnal; found singly, in pairs or small groups. **Food:** Insects. **Spoor:** Three short, forward-pointing toes; hind toe is absent.

Francolins   *Family Phasianidae*

Swainson's francolin

Cryptically coloured terrestrial or ground-living game birds. **Size:** 28–42 cm. **Habitat:** Bushveld, grass and thickets at edges of woodland; cultivated lands, savanna, riverine bush and vleis. **Habits:** Found singly, in pairs or in coveys of up to eight birds. Roosts in trees or on the ground at night. **Food:** Seeds, berries, roots, bulbs, insects, snails. **Spoor:** Three forward-pointing toes with angled backward pointing toe. Other signs: Loud alarm call.

Guineafowl

Family Numididae

Helmeted guineafowl

There are two species in this family in southern Africa. **Size:** 50–58 cm. **Habitat:** Helmeted guineafowl: open grassland, vleis, savanna, cultivated lands, edge of karoo scrub, bushveld. Crested guineafowl: montane, riparian, dune and coastal forests. **Habits:** Gregarious. **Food:** Seeds, bulbs, tubers, berries, insects, snails, ticks, millipedes, fallen grain. **Spoor:** Three forward-pointing toes and angled backward pointing toe.

Korhaans

Eupodotis species

Redcrested korhaan

Medium size birds with yellow legs, robust bodies, long necks, large heads and yellow legs. **Size:** Length 50–53 cm; mass 670–715 g. **Habitat:** Widespread. **Habits:** Usually solitary, sometimes found in pairs. **Food:** Mainly plant material; also insects. **Spoor:** Short, thick toes; hind toe absent.

Kori Bustard

Ardeotis kori

Nigel Dennis/SIL.

Louis Liebenberg

Said to be the heaviest of all flying birds; greyish brown above, with a white belly, neck and a breast which is finely barred (though it looks grey from a distance). The head is slightly crested with a longish bill. **Size:** 1.2–1.50 m. **Habitat:** Open plains of the Karoo, highveld grassland, Kalahari sandveld, arid scrub, Namib Desert, lightly wooded savanna, bushveld. **Habits:** Found solitary or in pairs when breeding, otherwise gregarious, gathering in flocks of up to 40 or more individuals. **Food:** Insects, small vertebrates, carrion, seeds, gum. **Spoor:** Long legs with short, thick toes; the hind toe is absent.

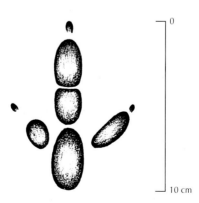

0

10 cm

Blue Crane
Anthropoides paradiseus

This beautiful bird is a uniform blue-grey in colour, with long slate-grey tail feathers curving to the ground. **Size:** 1.02–1.07 m. **Habitat:** Midland and highland grassveld, fringes of Karoo, cultivated land, edges of vleis. **Habits:** Highly gregarious when not breeding, otherwise found in pairs or family groups. **Food:** Frogs, reptiles, insects, fish, grain, green shoots, grass seeds. **Spoor:** Long legs, but short toes; the hind toe is reduced and elevated.

Redknobbed Coot
Fulica cristata

A medium-sized bird, black with white bill and frontal shield backed by two dark red knobs. **Size:** 43 cm. **Habitat:** Inland waters. **Habits:** Spends most of its time in open water. **Food:** Water plants, grass, insects and seeds. **Spoor:** A distinctive track, created by the scalloped webbing on the toes. The hind toe is angled slightly. Other signs: Very large mound-like nests of aquatic vegetation. Eggs are laid on top.

Ostrich
Struthio camelus

Hein van Horsten/SIL

Louis Liebenberg

The world's largest living bird. Males are black with white wings, females brownish grey. **Size:** Up to 2 m in height. **Habitat:** Bushveld to desert. **Habits:** Found in flocks of 30–40 birds when not breeding. **Food:** Grass, berries, seeds, succulent plants, small reptiles and insects. **Spoor:** Legs are very long with only two toes. Other signs: The eggs are unmistakable, large and laid in communal, earthen nests which will be defended by a single male. Ostriches also produce copious amounts of mixed liquid and solid waste. Like that of all birds, their urea stains the droppings white. The call is a deep boom, not unlike the roar of a lion (for which it is often mistaken). Incidental signs include large discarded feathers.

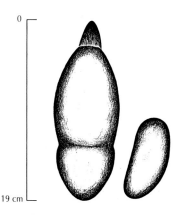

0

19 cm

Secretarybird   *Sagittarius serpentarius*

Peter Pickford/SIL

 A very large bird with long legs and tail. The body is mainly pale grey, with black belly, leg feathering, rump and crest feathers. The long crest is erectile. **Size:** 1.25–1.5 m in height. **Habitat:** Semidesert, grassland, savanna, open woodland, farmland, mountain slopes. **Habits:** Usually found in pairs, sometimes in groups of three or four. **Food:** Insects, rodents, frogs, toads, lizards and snakes, young hares, the young and eggs of various other birds. **Spoor:** Long legs, short toes webbed at the base, with strong claws. Other signs: The bird builds a large flat platform of sticks in the tops of dense thorn-trees.

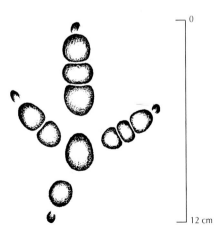

0

12 cm

Vultures   *Family Accipitridae*

Cape vulture

Southern Africa is home to nine species of these large, scavenging birds. They have very broad wings, enabling them to ride the thermals. Eyesight is highly developed; the head is usually naked of feathers to prevent fouling while feeding. **Size:** 64–120 cm. **Habitat:** Widely distributed across the northern parts of the subcontinent; the Cape vulture's range extends to the southern coast. **Habits:** Most visible when they soar above the plains in search of carrion, coming together in a feeding frenzy when a carcass is spotted. **Food:** Carrion and bone fragments. **Spoor:** All vultures leave similar spoor (though track sizes differ), most easily seen around a carcass. Other signs: Nests are usually built, of twigs and branches, on the tops of trees; Cape and bearded vultures nest on cliff ledges. Spoor size varies according to species.

Herons
Family Ardeidae

0

15 cm

Peter Pickford/SIL

Grey heron

Fairly large birds with slender necks and sharp beaks. **Size:** 97–140 cm. **Habitat:** Open grassland, the edges of inland waters, forest clearings. **Habits:** Herons wade in shallows to feed; solitary when feeding. **Food:** Frogs, fish, crabs, insects, rodents, small birds and reptiles, worms. **Spoor:** Three forward-pointing toes and a back toe slightly off centre.

Sacred Ibis
Threskiornis aethiopicus

0

14 cm

Nigel Dennis/SIL

One of four ibis species found in southern Africa, all with identical spoor. The sacred ibis is mainly white with black head and neck. **Size:** About 90 cm. **Habitat:** Varied; found in coastal lagoons, tidal flats, offshore islands; also inland downs. **Habits:** Forages and scavenges. **Food:** Diet includes insects, small mammals and birds, eggs, reptiles, carrion, seeds. **Spoor:** Legs are long, with toes partly webbed at base. Three toes point forward; backward pointing toe at a slight angle.

Egyptian Goose

Alopochen aegyptiacus

Nigel Dennis/SIL

 A large water bird, brown above, greyish below, with dark-brown patches around the eyes and on the centre of the breast, and a dark brown collar on the neck. In flight the wings are white with black primaries and green trailing edge. **Size:** 63–73 cm. **Habitat:** Most inland waters – rivers, dams, floodplains, pans, marshes; also estuaries, coastal lakes, cultivated fields. **Habits:** Highly gregarious. Young chicks will follow their mothers everywhere, and have been known to jump and 'parachute' down from great heights – from the trees or the buildings where they have built nests, for example, to be with her. **Food:** Grass and leaves, seeds, grain, crop seedlings, aquatic rhizomes, tubers. **Spoor:** The front toes of the bird are webbed; hind toes reduced.

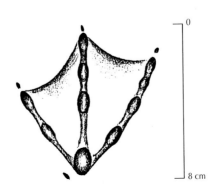

0

8 cm

Rats and Mice   *Families Cricetidae and Muridae*

Striped mouse

Example of the jumping spoor

These rodents vary considerably in habits and habitat: most of them are terrestrial, others burrow; most are nocturnal, although a few, like the striped mouse *Rhabdomys pumilio*, are active during the day. **Size:** From about 10 cm head-to-tail up to the giant rat's 80 cm. **Habitat:** Varied; nests may be in underground burrows, in piles of vegetation, in rock crevices, or in holes in tree-trunks. **Habits:** There are both solitary and gregarious forms. **Food:** A variety of plant material, invertebrates, small snakes and lizards, birds' eggs and nestlings. **Spoor:** Four toes show in the fore footprints, five toes in the hind footprints. When jumping, the hind prints appear ahead of the foreprints (see illustration, below).

hind feet

forefeet

Ground Squirrel *Xerus inauris*

Nigel Dennis/SIL

The upper parts of this rodent are cinnamon in colour, but individuals vary in shade. The belly is usually tinged buff; with lateral stripes running along either side of the body. **Size:** Height 24 cm; tail 21 cm; mass 600 g. **Habitat:** Is found throughout the more arid parts of the subregion; the animal has a preference for open terrain with sparse bush cover. **Habits:** Diurnal and terrestrial; gregarious; colonies of up to about 30 live in warrens with many entrances. **Food:** Mainly vegetarian; diet includes leaves and stems of grasses, seeds, bulbs, roots and plant stems; some insect food. **Spoor:** The ground squirrel has five toes on the forefoot, the first of which is rudimentary and without a claw; the hind foot also has five toes. Claws are long (about 10 mm), sharp, slightly curved.

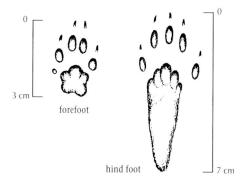

forefoot

hind foot

Tree Squirrel

Paraxerus cepapi

Nigel Dennis/SIL

 The species varies greatly in size and colour: pale grey overall in the western parts of its range, darker, more buffy, sometimes rusty in the east. **Size:** Height 18 cm; tail 17 cm; mass 200 g. **Habitat:** Savanna woodland of various types. **Habits:** Generally solitary, but also occurs in pairs or in groups comprising female with two or three young. The animal is both arboreal and terrestrial. **Food:** Predominantly vegetarian; diet includes flowers, leaves, seeds, berries, fruits and bark; also insects. The feeding sites are marked by accumulations of the discarded (inedible) remains of the meal. **Spoor:** The tree squirrel has four toes on the forefeet and five on the hind, each with short, sharp, curved claws adapted for arboreal life. The animal's trail nearly always starts and ends at the base of a tree; clawmarks can also be seen on the tree's bark.

0

2.5 cm

forefoot

0

4.5 cm

hind foot

42

Springhare   *Pedetes capensis*

Nigel Dennis

With its short front legs, long powerful hind legs and long tail, the springhare bears a striking resemblance to a miniature kangaroo. **Size:** Height 39 cm; tail 40 cm; mass 3.1 kg. **Habitat:** Widespread. **Habits:** Nocturnal; congregates in scattered groups when feeding; usually feeds within 250 m of burrow. **Food:** Mainly grass. **Spoor:** The springhare has five toes on the forefoot, with sharp, narrow, curved claws 18–20 mm in length over the curve. Five toes on the hind feet, the first absent from the spoor, the second, third and fourth elongated (the third is the longest). The fifth claw, which is the shortest, does not mark in the spoor except when the animal sits up, in which case the whole hind foot, right back to the ankle, may show in the spoor. The marks of the front claws, used in excavation, can often be seen on the sides of a burrow, but seldom show in the spoor since the springhare usually moves on the hind feet – that is, it hops, holding the forelegs close to the body.

Porcupine

Hystrix africaeaustralis

Anton Pauw

The largest African rodent, characterized by its armoury of erectile spines and quills. **Size:** Length 84 cm; mass 18 kg. **Habitat:** Occurs in most types of vegetation. Shelters often contain accumulations of bones (a source of phosphate). **Habits:** Almost exclusively nocturnal; usually solitary, occasionally found in pairs or in groups comprising female and young. Defends itself by rattling its quills to intimidate its attacker; also reverses into the intruder to dislodge barbed quills in its flesh. **Food:** Predominantly vegetarian; diet includes bulbs, tubers, roots, fallen wild fruits; also gnaws the bark of trees. **Spoor:** The porcupine has five toes on the front foot, the first toe reduced to a small stump without a claw. The other toes on the front feet have well- developed claws. Five toes on the hind foot, each with a claw; the fore- and hind feet each show three intermediate pads and two proximal pads in the spoor. The spoor also shows the marks of the quills, which are dragged. Other signs: One or more discarded quills.

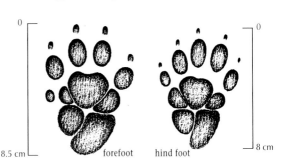

0   0

8.5 cm   8 cm

forefoot   hind foot

Hedgehog   *Atelerix frontalis*

Peter Pickford/SIL

A small, spiny insectivore. **Size:** 20 cm in length; mass 400 g. **Habitat:** A wide variety of habitats, including scrub bush and grassland. **Habits:** Predominantly nocturnal; rests by day curled up in debris in the shade of bushes, grass or holes. Has an acute sense of smell, but eyesight is poor. Usually slow in its movements; defends itself by rolling up into a ball; alarm call a high-pitched scream. **Food:** Beetles, termites, centipedes, millipedes, grasshoppers, moths, earthworms, small mice, lizards, frogs, slugs, eggs and the chicks of terrestrial birds, plus some vegetable matter. **Spoor:** The hedgehog has five toes on the front foot, the first of which shows behind the intermediate pad in the spoor; the hind foot has four toes, which are often dragged, leaving characteristic drag-marks in the sand.

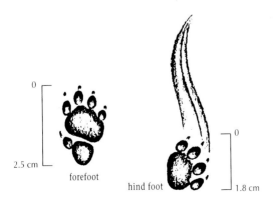

0
2.5 cm

forefoot

hind foot

0
1.8 cm

Hares

Family Leporidae

Scrub hare

Southern Africa supports two species: the scrub hare *Lepus saxatilis*, and the Cape hare *Lepus capensis*. The former has grizzled greyish or buffy upperparts, while the Cape hare is a light buff in colour, grizzled with black ticking in the southwestern Cape and a lighter whitish grey with greyish ticking in Botswana.

Size: Length 45–60 cm; mass 1.5–4.5 kg. **Habitat:** Distributional ranges overlap, but there are marked differences between the habitat requirements of the two species. The Cape hare prefers dry, open country (notably grassland plains); the scrub hare, scrub or woodland. **Habits:** Predominantly nocturnal; hares lie up during the day in grass clumps or under small bushes, which creates depressions or forms with a characteristic shape. They are for the most part solitary. **Food:** Leaves, stems and rhizomes of dry and green grass. The Cape hare favours areas with short grass, green grass and fresh green shoots. **Spoor:** These animals, which leave a characteristic bounding trail (see illustration), have a thick mass of hair beneath their feet, so the pad imprints are not well defined. Four claws may show in the spoor of the fore- and hind feet.

left hind foot

right hind foot

0

4 cm

right forefoot

left forefoot

0

3.5 cm

Rock Hyrax (Dassie)   *Procavia capensis*

 The upperparts of this little animal vary in colour from yellowish buff to reddish or greyish brown; the appearance is generally grizzled. **Size:** Length 45–60 cm; mass 2.5–4.6 kg. **Habitat:** The rock dassie occurs only in rocky outcrops.

Habits: Active mainly during the day; will move 50 or 100 m on flat ground to feed. **Food:** A browser in some parts of the region, predominantly a grazer in other parts. **Spoor:** The dassie has four toes on the front feet and three on the hind. All the toes have nails except the inner one on the hind foot, which has a curved grooming claw that shows in the print. Other signs: Urinates and defecates in latrines.

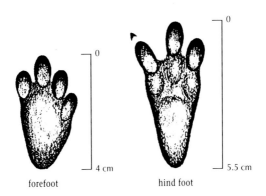

forefoot   hind foot

Pangolin

Manis temminckii

Nigel Dennis/SIL

 An unusual animal, armoured with sharp-edged scales. **Size:** Length 70–100 cm; mass 5–15 kg. **Habitat:** Savanna. **Habits:** Solitary; predominantly nocturnal. Under severe stress it curls up into a tight ball. **Food:** Ants and termites. **Spoor:** Five toes on the forefeet, the first with a small nail, the central three with long, strongly curved claws. Five toes on the hind feet, each with a short nail-like claw which marks in the spoor. When walking, the body is balanced on the hind feet, with the forefeet and tail held clear of the ground. The spoor shows the rounded pads of the hind feet with, usually, four nails touching the ground, the occasional scrape of the tail and the mark of the front edges of the long, curved front claws. Other signs: Droppings are usually composed of sand and the remains of ants and termites.

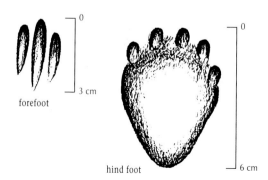

forefoot

hind foot

48

Lesser Bushbaby

Galago moholi

Peter Pickford/SIL

This little prosimian primate has huge eyes and large ears. Coloration: upperparts are light grey or grey-brown, the underparts are somewhat lighter. **Size:** Length 30–40 cm; mass 120–210 g. **Habitat:** Savanna woodland. **Habits:** Nocturnal; rests by day in family groups of two to seven, foraging alone by night. May construct a platform-like nest. **Food:** Lives on a diet of gum, augmented by insects. **Spoor:** Five digits on each foot, with soft, enlarged pads under the tip of each. Apart from the second digit of the hind foot, which has a curved grooming claw, each digit has a small nail. On the ground it moves by hopping on its hind legs, the forelimbs making no contact with the ground.

left hind foot   right hind foot

Vervet Monkey

Cercopithecus aethiops

Nigel Dennis/SIL

This little black-faced primate's upperparts are grizzled, the underparts whitish. **Size:** Length 95–130 cm; mass 3.5–8 kg. **Habitat:** Mainly savanna woodland. **Habits:** Diurnal; active from dawn till mid-morning, when it rests in a sheltered area until early in the afternoon (in hot weather), after which it continues foraging. Spends much of its time in trees searching for wild fruits, but also feeds on the ground. Troops comprise up to 20 members. **Food:** The vervet monkey is for the most part a vegetarian, living on wild fruits, flowers, leaves, seeds and seed pods. It also eats insects. **Spoor:** Thumb and big toe are fully opposable; each finger and toe has a nail. The feet are larger than the hands.

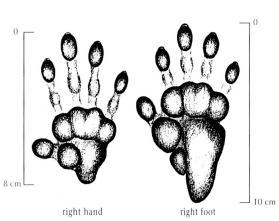

right hand right foot

Samango Monkey

Cercopithecus mitis

Rod Haester/Photo Access

The samango is much darker in colour than the vervet monkey, has a dark brown (not black) face and long cheek-hairs. **Size:** Length 1–1.4 m; mass 4–10 kg. **Habitat:** Forest. **Habits:** Diurnal; active from or just before sunrise, rests during the hottest hours of the day. Troop size varies from four individuals to more than 30. **Food:** Mainly fruits, dry and green leaves, flowers, pods and shoots; also insects. **Spoor:** Identical to that of the vervet monkey, with five fingers on each hand, five toes on each foot.

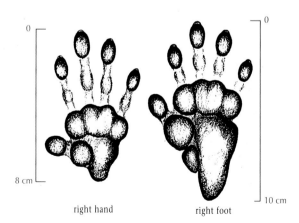

right hand   right foot

Chacma Baboon   *Papio cynocephalus*

Nigel Dennis/SIL

 This is the largest of southern Africa's primates (other than humans). Chacma baboons are formidable, especially the males: their canines are longer than those of the lion. **Size:** Length 1–1.6 m; mass 25–45 kg. **Habitat:** Widely distributed; primarily savanna environment but also in mountainous areas and on forest fringes. **Habits:** A gregarious species; usually associated with impala herds; troops may number up to 100 individuals. Diurnal; at night they sleep on high krantzes or in trees with thick foliage. **Food:** Omnivorous; diet includes grasses, seeds, roots, bulbs, leaves, flowers, wild fruits, pods and shoots. Turns over stones in search of insects, arachnids and slugs. **Spoor:** The thumb and big toe are fully opposable; each finger and toe has a nail. The feet are twice as long as the hands. Other signs include a very loud bark when alarmed or excited.

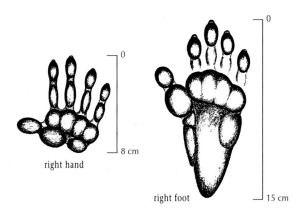

right hand

right foot

Cape Clawless Otter

Aonyx capensis

 The largest of Africa's otters. The upperparts vary from light to very dark brown, the underparts are lighter in colour. **Size:** Length 1.1–1.6 m; mass 10–18 kg. **Habitat:** A predominantly aquatic species. Needs fresh water, even in coastal areas.

Habits: Generally solitary, but also seen in pairs and family parties. Mainly crepuscular. **Food:** Mostly crabs, frogs and fish. **Spoor:** The otter has five toes on each of the fore- and hind feet. The toes, adapted for feeling and grasping, have no claws on the forefeet and only rudimentary nails on the hind feet. In soft mud, the five toes, the intermediate pads and the proximal pads show clearly in the spoor. Latrines, situated near water, are characterized by crabshell remains and fish scales. The droppings can be distinguished from those of the water mongoose (see page 64), whose scats contain rodent fur and other items not normally eaten by otters. Identification is difficult where both species are feeding extensively on crabs alone. The water mongoose, however, invariably leaves the shell of the carapace.

0

0

forefoot   hind foot

11 cm   12 cm

Spotted-necked Otter   *Lutra maculicollis*

Pat de la Harpe/RDPL

A much smaller and slimmer animal than the Cape clawless otter (see page 53). Colour varies from chocolate brown to a deep, rich, reddish brown; the throat and upper chest mottled with white or creamy white. **Size:** 1 m; mass 3–5 kg. **Habitat:** An aquatic species, closely confined to large rivers, lakes and swamps. **Habits:** Usually found solitary or in family parties. Apparently crepuscular. **Food:** Mainly fish, but also crabs, freshwater molluscs; some birds and insects. **Spoor:** The otter has five toes on the fore- and hind feet; the feet are fully webbed. In soft mud the five toes, the intermediate pads and the proximal pads show clearly in the spoor. The front foot's claws, which are up to 1 cm over the curve, are light and very sharp; those on the back feet slightly shorter. You may find it difficult to discern the claw marks in soft mud, and only slight indications of the webs will be apparent, even on close inspection. Nor will the marks be clear on firm substrate. The spotted-necked otter defecates and urinates in secluded, sheltered latrines close to the water's edge.

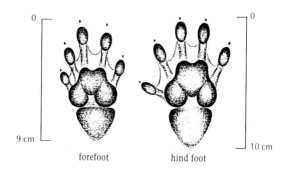

forefoot   hind foot

54

Honey Badger

Mellivora capensis

Lex Hes

This stocky, short-legged badger has a broad, light-coloured saddle which runs from above the eyes to the base of the tail, the colour contrasting with the black lower parts of the body. **Size:** Length 90–100 cm; mass 8–14 kg. **Habitat:** The animal has a wide habitat tolerance (it is found everywhere except in true desert. **Habits:** Predominantly nocturnal; generally solitary, though two or more individuals may hunt together. The animal is normally shy and retiring but it has a well deserved reputation for ferocity and fearlessness. When under stress it may secrete a strong-smelling fluid. **Food:** Omnivorous; diet includes scorpions, spiders, mice, lizards, centipedes, grasshoppers, small birds, snakes, berries, fruit, bee larvae and honey. **Spoor:** Five toes on both fore- and hind feet; the claws on the front foot are elongated and powerful; the hind-foot claws are much shorter. The intermediate pads are fused; a proximal pad on each of the fore- and hind feet is characteristic of the spoor.

0

0

forefoot

hind foot

11 cm

8 cm

Striped Weasel

Poecilogale albunicha

Nigel Dennis

A slender, sinuous little animal with a bushy tail and four distinctively white, longitudinal stripes on the jet-black fur. **Size:** Length 40–50 cm; mass 200–350 g. **Habitat:** A savanna species, largely associated with grassland.

Habits: Striped weasels are mainly nocturnal; generally solitary but also found in pairs and family parties. **Food:** Carnivorous, feeding on prey such as mice. **Spoor:** Five toes on the fore- and hind feet; the claws on the front foot are strongly curved and longer than those on the hind. The proximal pad of the forefoot may sometimes appear in the spoor; the hind-foot spoor will show the outer four toes and claws. The first toe or claw, or both, may also show.

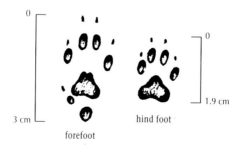

0

3 cm

forefoot

0

1.9 cm

hind foot

Striped Polecat   *Ictonyx striatus*

Chris & Tilde Stuart

A small black animal with distinctive longitudinal white stripes on the sides of its body. The
tail is mostly white. **Size:** Length 57–67 cm; mass
600–1,400 g. **Habitat:** The species has a wide
habitat tolerance. **Habits:** Nocturnal, terrestrial
and solitary, although one can occasionally see pairs and females
with young. If cornered, the polecat will turn its hindquarters to
the aggressor and eject a pungent secretion from its anal glands.
Food: Mainly insects and mice. **Spoor:** Five toes on the fore- and
hind feet. The forefoot's claws are strong, curved and long (up to
18 mm over the curve); those of the hind feet are much shorter. All
five toes and claws on the fore- and hind feet mark in the spoor.
The forefoot's proximal pad does not show.

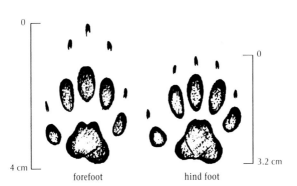

forefoot   hind foot

African Civet

Civettictis civeta

The civet has a greyish or whitish shaggy coat with black spots on the body, black stripes on the tail and neck. The lower parts of the legs are black, the tail bushy. **Size:** Length 1.2–1.4 m; mass 9–15 kg. **Habitat:** Well-watered savanna and forest. **Habits:** Predominantly nocturnal; generally solitary. **Food:** Omnivorous; diet includes insects, wild fruit, mice, reptiles, birds, amphibia, myriapods (centipedes and millipedes), arachnids and carrion. **Spoor:** Five toes on fore- and hind feet, but only four show in the spoor. The claws make clear marks. The animal deposits its faeces in latrines (or 'civetrenes').

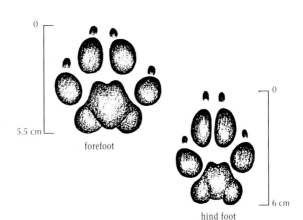

forefoot

hind foot

Small-spotted Genet   *Genetta genetta*

Nigel Dennis/SIL

Distinguished from the large-spotted genet (see page 60) by a crest of black hair along the back, a longer and coarser coat, more black on the hind feet, darker body spots and (usually) a white-tipped tail. Its sharp, curved, extendible claws do not show in the spoor. **Size:** Length 86–100 cm; mass 1.5–2.6 kg. **Habitat:** The more open areas of savanna woodland, dry grassland and dry vlei areas. **Habits:** Nocturnal; mainly solitary, but also found in pairs. **Food:** Small rodents, birds, reptiles, insects, spiders and scorpions. **Spoor:** Identical to large-spotted genet. Five toes on fore- and hind feet; the first is set back and does show in the footprints; nor do the sharp, curved, extendible claws.

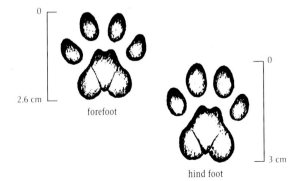

0

2.6 cm

forefoot

0

3 cm

hind foot

Large-spotted Genet
Genetta tigrina

Chris & Tilde Stuart

Similar to the small-spotted genet (see page 59) but lacks the spinal crest and has a black-tipped tail. The spots on the body are generally larger than those of its small-spotted cousin. **Size:** Length 85–110 cm; mass 1.5–3.2 kg. **Habitat:** Associated with well-watered country; its presence in arid regions is usually confined to riverine strips. **Habits:** Nocturnal; mainly solitary, but also found in pairs. **Food:** Rats, mice, insects, ground birds, arachnids, reptiles and wild fruit. **Spoor:** Identical to small-spotted genet (see page 59). Shows four toes in the spoor.

Louis Liebenberg

0

0

2.6 cm

3 cm

forefoot   hind foot

Large Grey Mongoose   *Herpestes ichneumon*

A grey animal covered by coarse fur and a long tail with a distinctive black tip. Lower parts of the legs are black. **Size:** Length 1–1.1 m; mass 2.5–4 kg. **Habitat:** Closely associated with water; occurs in riverine forest or bush, or indeed any thick cover near fresh water. **Habits:** Mainly diurnal; solitary individuals and family groups of up to five individuals may also be seen. **Food:** Frogs, fish, crabs, murids (mice), birds, reptiles, insects. Also reputed to raid poultry. **Spoor:** Five toes on the fore- and hind foot. The first toe of the forefoot is small and located behind the intermediate pad; the forefoot's other four toes have long claws that mark clearly in the spoor. The proximal pad of the forefoot shows in the spoor when the animal is moving slowly but may not do so when it is trotting or running. The first toe of the hind foot does not usually show, but the first claw may mark in the footprint. The other four toes have claws, which are shorter than those of the forefoot and mark clearly in the spoor.

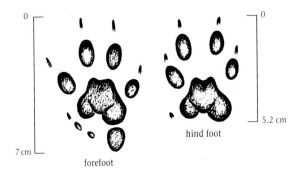

0   0

5.2 cm

hind foot

7 cm

forefoot

Slender Mongoose

Galerella sanguinea

Clem Haagner/Gallo Images

A small, slender animal with a long tail which has a characteristic black tip. Body colour varies, ranging from reddish, yellowish and greyish to a dark brown that looks black in the field. **Size:** Length 50–65 cm; mass 700–900 g. **Habitat:** The slender mongoose has a wide habitat tolerance. **Habits:** Terrestrial and solitary; predominantly diurnal. It shelters in disused antbear holes or holes in termitaria. **Food:** Mainly insects; also scorpions, centipedes, wild fruits, lizards, rodents, birds, snakes, frogs, **Spoor:** Five toes on the forefoot, the first small and located behind the intermediate pad. Except in soft substrate, the first toe does not (usually) mark in the spoor. The proximal pad of the forefoot, which may show when the animal is moving slowly or in soft substrate, does not show when it is trotting or running. The claws are sharp. The hind foot has five toes, each with a sharp, curved claw; four toes show in the spoor; the fifth doesn't show but its claw may.

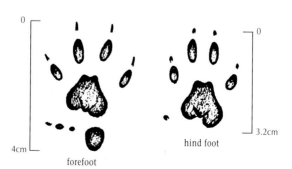

forefoot

hind foot

Small Grey Mongoose   *Galerella pulverulenta*

Chris & Tilde Stuart

A small, slim animal, but heavier and more stoutly built than the slender mongoose (see opposite). Its general colour is speckled grey. **Size:** Length 55–69 cm; mass 500 g–1 kg. **Habitat:** The species has a wide habitat tolerance. **Habits:** Diurnal; normally solitary, occasionally found in pairs. **Food:** Mainly insects, but also fruit, carrion, rats and mice, reptiles and ground birds, their eggs and young. **Spoor:** Five toes on the forefeet, the first small and located behind the intermediate pad. Except in soft substrate, the first toe does not usually mark in the spoor. The proximal pad of the forefoot, which may show when the animal is moving slowly or in soft substrate, does not mark when it is trotting or running. The hind foot has five toes, but the first toe does not show, although its claw may. The other four toes each have a sharp, curved claw.

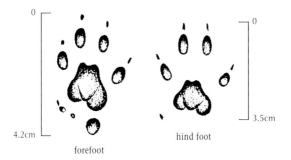

forefoot   hind foot

4.2cm   3.5cm

Water Mongoose

Atilax paludinosus

A robust mongoose with a coarse, shaggy coat and tapering tail. Usually dark brown in colour. **Size:** Length 80–100 cm; mass 2.5–5.5 kg. **Habitat:** Associated with well-watered terrain; found near rivers, streams, marshes, swamps, vleis, dams and tidal estuaries. **Habits:** Crepuscular. Normally solitary; adult females may be accompanied by juveniles. **Food:** Frogs, crabs, rodents, fish, insects, freshwater mussels and vegetable matter. **Spoor:** Five toes on the fore- and hind feet, the first small and showing in the spoor behind the intermediate pads. The other four toes are long and finger-like, and tend to splay. Claws on the front feet are stout and curved; those on the back are slightly longer. The proximal pad of the front foot, which may show in the spoor when the animal is moving slowly, may not mark at speed. Dry carapaces of crabs left on river banks are an indication of this mongoose's presence.

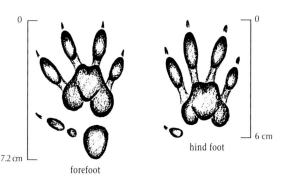

forefoot

hind foot

Dwarf Mongoose

Helogale parvula

Nigel Dennis/SIL

Africa's smallest mongoose. At a distance the general colour, a uniform speckled brown, appears very dark brown. **Size:** Length 35–40 cm; mass 220–350 g. **Habitat:** Favours dry, open woodland or grassland. **Habits:** Active only when the sun is well up. Lives in troops of 8–10 individuals; groups take up permanent residence, usually in termite mounds. **Food:** Mainly insectivorous; also eats snails, earthworms, reptiles, eggs of ground birds and snakes. **Spoor:** Five toes on the forefoot, the first small and located behind the intermediate pad. The front foot's first toe and proximal pad, which may show when the animal is moving slowly, may not show at speed. The hind foot has five toes but the first toe doesn't show, although its claw may, positioned well behind the other four toes. The claws of the front feet are long, curved and sharp; those on the hind feet are shorter.

0

forefoot

3.4 cm

0

hind foot

2.5 cm

Banded Mongoose

Mungos mungo

Peter Pickford/SIL

A small mongoose with a coarse, wiry, brownish grey coat. Distinguished by its short, tapering tail and the dozen or so black transverse bands on its back. **Size:** Length 50–65 cm; mass 1–1.6 kg. **Habitat:** Wide habitat tolerance. **Habits:** Diurnal; gregarious; lives in troops that vary in size from a few to more than 30 individuals. **Food:** Insects, grubs, myriapods, snails, small reptiles, the eggs and young of ground-nesting birds, wild fruits; also scorpions and spiders. **Spoor:** Five toes on the forefoot, the first one small and located behind the intermediate pad. The forefoot's first toe and proximal pad, which may show when the animal is moving slowly, may not do so at speed. Five toes on the hind foot, but the first toe doesn't show, only its claw may, well behind the other four toes. The claws of the front feet are long and sharply curved; those of the back feet are rather shorter.

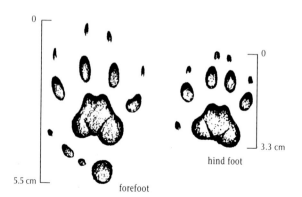

hind foot

forefoot

White-tailed Mongoose   *Ichneumia albicauda*

A large, shaggy-coated mongoose, distinguished by its longish legs and a tail that is white for about four-fifths of its length. **Size:** Length range 90–150 cm; mass range 3.5–5.2 kg.

Habitat: Associated with savanna woodland in well-watered areas. **Habits:** Nocturnal; terrestrial (it cannot climb trees). Normally solitary, but also found in pairs and family parties. **Food:** Mainly insects; also vegetable matter, millipedes, spiders, scorpions, reptiles, frogs, murids (mice). **Spoor:** Five toes on the fore- and hind feet, but the first toes do not show in the spoor. The first claw of the forefoot marks well behind the other four toes; the first claw of the hind foot barely touches the ground. The forefoot's claws are broad, strong and curved; those on the back feet are about the same length but narrower and straighter.

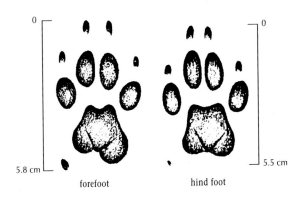

forefoot   hind foot

Yellow Mongoose

Cynictis penicillata

Nigel Dennis/SIL

A small mongoose with a short, pointed muzzle. Its colour varies from a richly coloured tawny-yellowish in the southern parts of the range to grizzled and greyish in the north. The former has a long, white-tipped tail and long-haired coat, the latter a shorter tail without the white tip. **Size:** Length 40–60 cm; mass 4.5–9 kg. **Habitat:** Prefers open country. **Habits:** Predominantly diurnal; gregarious, living in warrens in colonies of up to 20 or more individuals. **Food:** Mainly insectivorous, but also takes mice, small birds, reptiles, scorpions, centipedes, spiders and frogs. **Spoor:** Five toes on the forefoot and four on the hind. The forefoot's first toe is set well behind the other four and does not mark in the spoor; nor, usually, does the claw of the first toe. The other four toes have long claws; those on the hind feet are shorter.

forefoot   hind foot

Suricate

Suricata suricatta

Jéan du Plessis

A small, attractive mongoose with conspicuous black rings around the eyes and a slender, tapering, black-tipped tail. Its general colour is a light grizzled fawn with dark brown transverse bands on the back. The animal is commonly known as the meerkat. **Size:** Length 45–55 cm; mass 6.2–9.6 kg. **Habitat:** Occurs throughout the southwestern arid zone. **Habits:** Diurnal; gregarious; lives in warrens with several entrances, in colonies of up to 30 individuals. **Food:** Mainly insects; also scorpions, spiders, millipedes, centipedes, and small reptiles. **Spoor:** Four toes on the fore- and hind feet. The claws on the front feet are strong and curved; the back ones are much shorter.

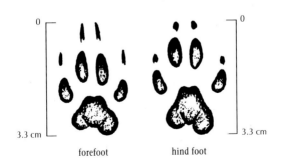

forefoot   hind foot

Bat-eared Fox   *Otocyon megalotis*

Nigel Dennis/SIL

 This attractive animal, which looks rather like a small jackal, has large, black-edged ears, blackish legs and a bushy, black-tipped tail. The overall colour is silvery buffy grey. **Size:** Length 75–90 cm; mass 3–5 kg. **Habitat:** Especially associated with open country within the southwest arid and southern savanna zones. **Habits:** Both diurnal and nocturnal. **Food:** Mainly insects, in particular the harvester termite; also scorpions, murids (mice), reptiles, spiders, millipedes, centipedes and wild fruit. **Spoor:** Five toes on the forefoot, the first located far back so that it does not mark in the spoor. The claws on the forefeet are long and slightly curved. Four toes on the hind feet, with short claws. The holes which it digs when feeding are characteristically narrow and deep.

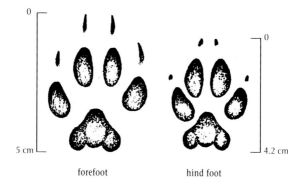

forefoot   hind foot

Cape Fox

Vulpes chama

Nigel Dennis/SIL

A small fox with large, pointed ears, and a short, pointed muzzle. Its upperparts appear silvery grey, the underparts pale buffy. The bushy tail is pale fawn with a black tip. **Size:** Length 86–97 cm; mass 2.5–4 kg. **Habitat:** Associated with open grassland country. **Habits:** Mainly nocturnal; generally solitary; found throughout the drier parts of southern Africa. **Food:** Predominantly mice and insects; also small mammals, scorpions, spiders, centipedes, birds and eggs, reptiles, carrion, wild fruit and green grass; sometimes accused of killing lambs. **Spoor:** Five toes on the forefoot; the first toe and claw do not mark in the spoor. Four toes on the hind foot. The claws on both the front and hind feet are thin and sharp.

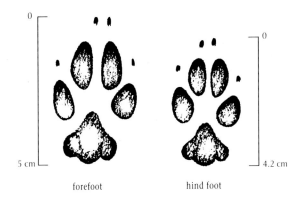

forefoot   hind foot

Black-backed Jackal   *Canis mesomelas*

Nigel Dennis/SIL

This animal has a reddish-brown body colour, a black saddle on the back, and a bushy, black-tipped tail. **Size:** Length 96–110 cm; mass 6–10 kg. **Habitat:** Wide tolerance. **Habits:** Both diurnal and nocturnal; found alone, in pairs and family parties. **Food:** Mainly carrion, but also small mammals such as rats and mice; insects, vegetable matter, birds, reptiles, sun spiders, scorpions, centipedes and green grass. **Spoor:** Five toes on the forefoot; the first toe, which carries the dew claw, is set well back and does not mark in the spoor. The hind feet have four toes. The claws are relatively short. The black-backed jackal normally moves at a trot, leaving a trail in which both forefoot tracks lie on one side and both hind foot tracks on the other.

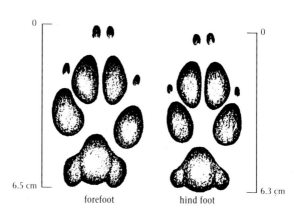

forefoot   hind foot

Side-striped Jackal   *Canis adustus*

C. F. Bartlett/Photo Access

A large jackal, overall grey or greyish buff in colour with a white-tipped tail and a faint black-and-white stripe along the side. **Size:** Length 96–120 cm; mass 7.5–12 kg. **Habitat:** Avoids open savanna grassland, favouring more thickly wooded country. **Habits:** Nocturnal; found alone, in pairs and family parties. **Food:** Mainly vegetable matter, including wild fruits; also small mammals (predominantly rats and mice), insects, carrion, birds and reptiles. **Spoor:** Five toes on the front foot; the first toe, which carries the dew claw, is located far back and does not show in the spoor. Four toes on the hind feet.

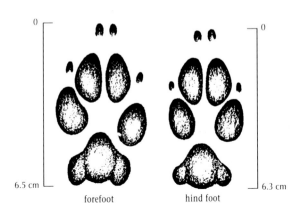

0			0
6.5 cm			6.3 cm
	forefoot	hind foot	

Wild Dog

Lycaon pictus

Nigel Dennis/SIL

 A dog-like animal in appearance, its body is blotched with black, yellow and white. It has large, rounded ears and a white-tipped bushy tail. **Size:** Length 1.05–1.5 m; mass 20–30 kg.
Habitat: Associated with open plains and open savanna woodland. **Habits:** Adapted to living in packs of about 10–15 individuals, though pack size can be up to 50. Hunts by sight, normally in the early morning and late evening. Generally active only during daylight hours. **Food:** Mainly the smaller to medium-sized antelope; also hares and the young of the larger bovids. **Spoor:** Four toes on the fore- and hind feet, each carrying short, powerful claws.

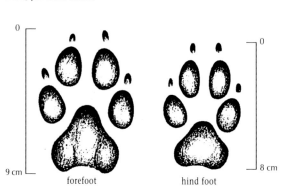

forefoot   hind foot

Aardwolf *Proteles cristatus*

The aardwolf is about the size of a jackal but hyaena-like in shape, with shoulders sloping down to the back legs. It has a thick-haired mane on its back and a bushy, black-tipped tail. The general colour is yellowish brown or buff, with vertical stripes on the body. **Size:** Length 84–100 cm; mass 6–11 kg. **Habitat:** Wide tolerance. **Habits:** Predominantly nocturnal; normally solitary, but sometimes found in pairs or family parties. **Food:** Mainly termites; also other insects, spiders and millipedes. **Spoor:**

Five toes on the forefoot; the first toe is located high up and does not mark in the spoor. Four toes on the hind feet. The claws are narrow. The animal defecates within oval-shaped middens; the faeces are covered up by scraping with the front feet.

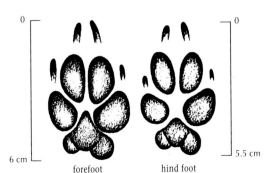

0   0

6 cm   5.5 cm

forefoot   hind foot

Brown Hyaena

Hyaena brunnea

A shy animal, in profile higher at the shoulders than at the rump. Has a long, shaggy brown coat, a lighter-coloured mantle and a long, bushy tail. **Size:** Length 1.3–1.6 m; mass 42–47 kg. **Habitat:** Desert, semidesert, open scrub, open woodland savanna. **Habits:** Mainly nocturnal; lies in groups but forages alone. **Food:** A scavenger, but also hunts small mammals, birds, reptiles. **Spoor:** Four toes on the fore- and hind feet, each with a short, heavy claw. Forefoot is much larger than the hind, distinguishing the brown hyaena's spoor from that of its spotted cousin (size difference is much less marked in the latter). Defecates in latrines.

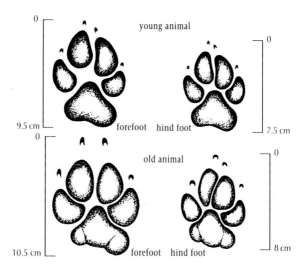

Spotted Hyaena   *Crocuta crocuta*

This tough, opportunistic carnivore's shoulders are heavier and stand much higher than its hindquarters; its dull yellowish coat is marked by irregular dark spots. **Size:** Length 1.2–1.8 m; mass 60–80 kg. **Habitat:** A savanna species associated with open plains, open woodland and semidesert scrub. **Habits:** Social organization is based on a matriarchal system of clans. Predominantly nocturnal, but also active by day. **Food:** Mainly large- or medium-sized ungulates, but will hunt or scavenge a wide range of other prey. **Spoor:** Four toes on the fore- and hind feet, each with a short, heavy claw. Spoor can be distinguished from that of the brown hyaena (see opposite page) by size difference between fore- and hind feet – a difference more marked in the brown hyaena. Territorial boundaries are carefully scent-marked with a creamy substance from the anal glands. Defecates in latrines.

forefoot   hind foot

Small Spotted Cat   *Felis nigripes*

Anthony Banister/Gallo Images

The smallest of the subregion's cats, generally tawny in colour, marked with large black spots and transverse stripes on the shoulder, with three black bands around the legs. The tail is bushy with black tip. **Size:** Length 50–63 cm; mass 1– 2 kg. **Habitat:** Associated especially with open country with some cover. **Habits:** Exclusively nocturnal; solitary. **Food:** Mainly murids (mice); also spiders, insects, reptiles and birds. **Spoor:** Footprints are much smaller than those of any other cats; spoor about the same size as the genet's (see page 59), though the shapes – of the toes and intermediate pads – are different.

Louis Liebenberg

Small spotted cat 'scats'

forefoot   hind foot

African Wild Cat   *Felis lybica*

Lex Hes

Looks very much like the domestic cat, but is slightly larger. The general colour ranges from greyish through buffish to ochre-like, with dark spots and stripes. **Size:** Length 85–100 cm; mass 2.5–6 kg. **Habitat:** Wide tolerance. **Habits:** Nocturnal; solitary. **Food:** Mainly rats and mice; also birds,

reptiles, insects, spiders and small mammals such as hares, springhares and the young of small antelope. **Spoor:** Footprints are similar in shape and size to those of the domestic cat. Like the latter, too, it excavates a depression to defecate, and carefully covers the scats by scraping with the front feet.

Louis Liebenberg

0 ⌐ ... 3.5 cm

0 ⌐ ... 3.8 cm

forefoot   hind foot

Serval   *Felis serval*

Nigel Dennis/SIL

A slender cat with long legs, small head, large ears and spotted and barred coat. The general colour is yellow with black spots. **Size:** Length 96–120 cm; mass 8–13 kg. **Habitat:** Confined to areas where there is permanent water; found in the higher rainfall areas. **Habits:** Serval are predominantly nocturnal; normally solitary, they are also sometimes seen in pairs and family groups (females with young). **Food:** They prey on mainly rats and mice; also other small mammals, birds, frogs, small reptiles, insects and sun spiders. **Spoor:** Footprints similar to those of the caracal (see opposite page), but narrower, the indentation at the front of the intermediate pad not as prominent. The serval drops scats randomly along paths, usually choosing a patch of short grass or a depression. It takes little or no trouble to cover the scats, making no more than a few quick scratches with the hind feet.

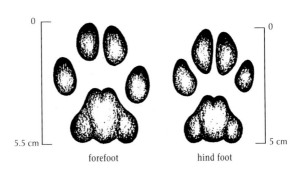

forefoot   hind foot

Caracal   *Felis caracal*

Nigel Dennis

A stockier cat than the serval (see opposite page) with shorter limbs, a short bushy tail and characteristic tufts on the ears. The overall colour is a reddish tan. **Size:** Length 70–110 cm; mass 7–19 kg. **Habitat:** Associated with open savanna woodland, open grassland and vleis. **Habits:** Mostly nocturnal; solitary. **Food:** Mainly small and medium-sized prey, which includes monkeys, the young of the larger antelopes, dassies, birds and reptiles. **Spoor:** Footprints are broader than those of the serval, and the indentation at the front of the intermediate pads is more prominent.

Louis Liebenberg

Note heavy indentation at front of pads.

forefoot   hind foot

Cheetah

Acinonyx jubatus

Nigel Dennis/SIL

A more slender animal than the leopard (see page 84), with longer legs, a much smaller head, and characteristic black 'tear marks' from the eye to the mouth. Its spots are also much smaller and more rounded than the leopard's rosettes.

Size: Length 1.8–2.2 m; mass 40–60 kg. **Habitat:** Open plains, the more open areas within savanna woodland, and the fringes of the desert. **Habits:** Predominantly diurnal; at its most active around sunrise and sunset; relies on speed to catch prey. Occurs in pairs or family parties of three or four, and to a lesser extent solitary

males. Groups numbering between 10 and 14 are sometimes seen in Namibia. **Food:** Mainly medium-sized or small bovids or the young of larger bovids; also terrestrial birds and small mammals such as hares and porcupines. **Spoor:** Unlike those of other cats, the cheetah's claws do not retract into sheaths but remain extended at all times. Longitudinal ridges beneath these high-speed predator's intermediate pads act like tyre-treads to prevent skidding.

Louis Liebenberg

An adult cheetah footprint: note the extended claws. Longitudinal ridges on the pads serve to prevent skidding.

0

10.5 cm

forefoot

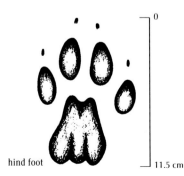

0

hind foot

11.5 cm

83

Leopard

Panthera pardus

Nigel Dennis/SIL

A more solid-bodied animal than the cheetah (see page 82), with shorter, stockier legs, and a larger head. Coloration: golden yellow, with distinct black, light-centred rosettes. **Size:** Length 1.6–2.1 m; mass 20–90 kg. **Habitat:** Wide tolerance. **Habits:** Solitary, except during mating season or when female is accompanied by young. Mainly nocturnal, with some diurnal activity in undisturbed areas. **Food:** Catholic diet includes small to medium-sized ungulates, on occasion larger mammals such as kudu and hartebeest, dassies, rats and mice, hares, birds, snakes, lizards, insects, scorpions, some of the smaller carnivores, occasionally baboons. Will also scavenge. **Spoor:** Male's footprints are larger and proportionately broader than those of the female. Female's toes are more slender. The leopard extends

Louis Liebenberg

The leopard's droppings: old (left) and new

Louis Liebenberg

Female

forefoot   hind foot

Male

forefoot   hind foot

its claws only when alarmed or charging. Other signs: Both males and females scent-mark by spraying urine. Leaves marks on trees where it has climbed or sharpened its claws. Traces of blood on the tree and animal remains indicate a carcass has been dragged up into the branches.

Lion
Panthera leo

Lanz van Hörsten/SIL

Largest of Africa's carnivores, sandy or tawny in colour; the males carry a mane of thick hair around the neck. **Size:** Length 2.5–3.3 m; mass 110–225 kg. **Habitat:** Wide tolerance. **Habits:** Mainly nocturnal; also active around sunrise and towards sunset and sometimes during daylight hours. The animal lives and hunts in prides which may number from a few individuals to 30 or more. Solitary males ousted from prides; solitary subadult males and females may also occur and tend to be nomadic. **Food:** Mainly medium-sized to large ungulates, but will kill a wide variety of mammals, from buffalo down to mice; also birds, reptiles and even insects. **Spoor:** The male's footprints are larger and proportionately broader than those of the female; the female's toes are more slender than those of the male (a young male's footprints may be the same size as a female's but can be distinguished by the shape). The claws are extended when charging, and show in the spoor. The lion scent-marks by spraying urine against shrubs, and at the same time makes scrape marks on the ground. It also sharpens its claws, and leaves claw marks, on the bark of trees.

Louis Liebenberg

Lion droppings

The spoor of an adult male lion

Young male

0   0

13 cm   12.5 cm

forefoot   hind foot

Adult male

0   0

14.5 cm   15 cm

forefoot   hind foot

Adult female

0   0

13 cm   12 cm

forefoot   hind foot

Elephant   *Loxodonta africana*

Lanz van Hörsten/SIL

The world's largest living land mammal, boasting a flexible and multipurpose trunk used for gathering its food, for sucking up water, greeting other elephants, chastening youngsters, smelling, trumpeting, breathing, and also as a weapon. **Size:** Shoulder height from 2.5–4 m; mass from 2.8–6.3 tons. **Habitat:** A wide habitat tolerance. **Habits:** Gregarious; the family groups comprise an adult female with her offspring or a number of closely related females with their offspring. Groups may come together to form herds. Bulls join the family herds only when a female is in oestrus. **Food:** Browse and graze. **Spoor:** Five hoofed toes on the front feet and four on the hind. The feet have a thick layer of cartilage, which acts as a shock absorber – and enables the elephant to move with minimal sound. The horny soles of the feet are cracked on the surface, the mosaic of cracks marking in the spoor. The random pattern of the cracks makes it possible for a trained tracker to identify individual elephants. The front feet are round and larger than the hind. Some trackers maintain that the hind feet of females, which are oval, are larger than those of males, but this needs to be confirmed. Elephants can be very destructive in their feeding habits, pushing over trees, pulling them up by the roots, or breaking off branches to get at young, fresh foliage. They also dig holes in sand, on river banks, to drink the clean, filtered water seeping through.

Hind footprint

Elephants dig holes for water

Droppings

Adult male

forefoot

hind foot

Adult female

forefoot

hind foot

Louis Liebenberg

89

White Rhinoceros
Ceratotherium simum

Characteristic features of this massive herbivore, also known as the square lipped rhino, include the square upper lip and a prominent hump above the shoulders. It is larger in size, and has a longer head, than its cousin the black (hook-lipped) rhinoceros (see page 92). **Size:** Shoulder height 1.8 m; mass 1.4–2.3 tons. **Habitat:** Areas of short grass, with adequately thick bush cover and fairly flat terrain. The white rhino is endangered; confined to reserves and other protected areas. **Habits:** The animal grazes at night, during the morning and in the late afternoon and evening, resting at intervals of a few hours. During the heat of the day it rests in shade. Occurs in small groups. **Food:** Grass. **Spoor:** Three toes, each with a broad, stout nail, on the fore- and hind feet. The nails are proportionately bigger, and gaps between them smaller than those of the black rhinoceros. The spoor of an adult is also bigger. Cushioned pads on the soles of the feet have a hard surface showing an intricate mosaic of irregular cracks – a random pattern

The white rhino's droppings

from which one can identify individuals. Other signs: The species has a preference for short grass, which it crops to within a centimetre of the ground. The bite width of an adult is about 20 cm. Dominant bulls habitually demarcate their territories with latrines and by spray-urinating along the boundaries. The dung of the white rhino contains grass.

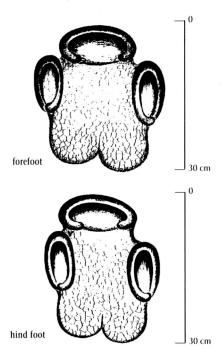

Black Rhinoceros   *Diceros bicornis*

Lex Hes

Also known as the hook-lipped rhino and distinguished from the white (square-lipped) rhinoceros (see page 90) by its smaller size, its pointed upper lip and its smaller head. **Size:** Shoulder height 1.6 m; mass 800–1,100 kg. **Habitat:** Needs an adequate supply of scrub and young trees on which to browse; also well-developed woodland or thickets where it can shelter during the heat of the day. The black rhino is highly endangered; confined to reserves and other protected areas. **Habits:** Solitary, or female with calf. Active during the early morning and late afternoon. **Food:** Mainly browse, but small quantities of grass are taken during the wet season. **Spoor:** Three toes, each with a broad, stout nail, on the fore- and hind feet. The nails are proportionately smaller than those of white rhino, the gaps between them bigger. The animal's spoor is also smaller than that of an adult white rhinoceros. Cushioned pads on the soles of the feet have a hard surface with a mosaic of irregular cracks, creating a random pattern in the spoor from which one can identify individual animals. A black rhino deposits dung in latrines, but will also defecate

Louis Liebenberg

randomly anywhere in its home range. It also sprays urine, kicks its dung about and spreads it around with its horn, all of which are signposts to its presence in an area. The dung contains twigs and the remains of leaves.

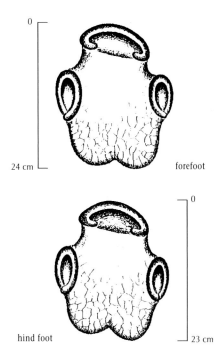

0

24 cm

forefoot

0

hind foot

23 cm

Burchell's Zebra   *Equus burchelli*

Nigel Dennis/SIL

This common relative of the horse can be distinguished from the two mountain zebras, *Equus zebra* (see opposite page) by the yellowish or greyish shadow stripes between the black on the hind-quarters, and also by the absence of a 'gridiron' pattern on top of the rump. **Size:** Shoulder height 1.3 m; mass 290–340 kg. **Habitat:** A savanna species, favouring areas of open woodland, open scrub and grassland. **Habits:** Generally active throughout the day. Gregarious; lives in small family groups. **Food:** Predominantly a grazer, but will sometimes browse and feed on herbs. **Spoor:** Hoof-prints are similar shape to, but much smaller than, those of adult horses; larger than those of domestic donkeys. Droppings have a regular kidney shape.

Louis Liebenberg

Zebra droppings

0   0

9.5 cm   10 cm

forefoot   hind foot

Mountain Zebras   *Equus zebra*

The two mountain zebras, which are very similar to each other, differ from Burchell's zebra in their smaller body size, in their black body stripes, which do not continue on to the white underparts, and in the lack of shadow stripes between them. The black markings on their rumps form a characteristic 'gridiron' pattern. **Size:** Shoulder height 1.3 m; mass 250–260 kg. **Habitat:** Historically, the Cape mountain zebra (subspecies *zebra*) occurred throughout the mountainous areas of the Cape (now seen in reserves such as the Mountain Zebra National Park), while Hartmann's mountain zebra (subspecies *hartmannae*) has been restricted to mountainous areas and flats in Namibia. **Habits:** Mainly diurnal; gregarious. **Food:** Predominantly a grazer, but will also browse. **Spoor:** An adult mountain zebra's hoofprints are smaller than those of adult Burchell's zebra. The hoofprints of the two subspecies of mountain zebra are identical but, as their distribution does not overlap, cannot be confused.

0   0

9 cm   10 cm
        forefoot   hind foot

Hippopotamus   *Hippopotamus amphibius*

Daryl Balfour/Gallo Images

This huge animal is especially adapted for its aquatic life: eyes, nose and ears all protrude from the water when the rest of the animal is submerged. **Size:** Shoulder height 1.5 m; mass 1–2 tons. **Habitat:** Needs open water in which it can totally submerge. **Habits:** A nocturnal feeder; rests by day partially submerged. Gregarious; occurs in herds (or schools), usually of between 10 and 15 individuals. **Food:** Grass. **Spoor:** Has

four toes, each with heavy broad nails, on the fore- and hind feet. Hippos tend to use established routes on dry land, the ground eventually being worn deeply into narrow paths. These are grooved on either side by the feet, leaving a narrow raised central ridge of loose soil. Territories are marked by piles of faeces, which the hippo scatters over a bush or stone by flicking its tail from side to side.

Louis Liebenberg

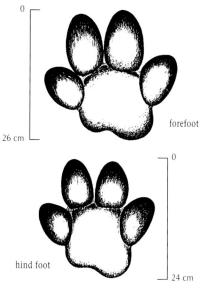

0

26 cm

forefoot

0

hind foot

24 cm

97

Giraffe   *Giraffa camelopardalis*

There are several varieties of this, the world's tallest animal, in Africa, each with a distinctive reticulate (net-like) pattern. The head has horny projections which the male uses, when fighting, to strike at the legs and neck of its opponent. On these occasions the two combatants stand side on and swing their long necks in wide arcs. The long, rough tongue enables the giraffe to grasp foliage and to strip the leaves of acacias; the copious, viscous saliva it produces helps it to swallow the thorns. The animal can gallop at up to 60 km/h but usually defends itself by kicking. **Size:** Shoulder height 3.9–5.2 m; mass 970–1,400 kg. **Habitat:** Associated with a wide variety of dry savanna ranging from scrub to woodland; often seen in company with zebra and wildebeest, who benefit from the giraffe's height and ability to survey the horizon. **Habits:** Predominantly diurnal. Gregarious; a loose herd structure comprises females and young, bachelor or mixed groups. Bulls are for the most part solitary. **Food:** Browser; favours acacia leaves and flowers. **Spoor:** Footprints are much larger and longer than those of any other of the cloven-hoofed animals. Droppings have one pointed end, an indentation at the blunt end, and are usually scattered by the height from which they fall. Saliva in the upper parts of trees may indicate the animal's very recent precence.

Droppings are usually scattered

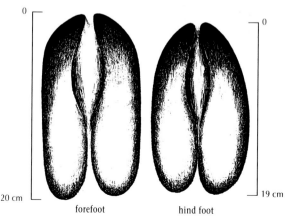

0

0

20 cm

19 cm

forefoot

hind foot

Warthog
Phacochoerus aethiopicus

An unmistakable pig-like animal with characteristic tusks, and wart-like protuberances on the face. Skin colour, often determined by the colour of the mud in which it wallows, is generally grey. **Size:** Shoulder height 70 cm; mass 60–105 kg. **Habitat:** Grassland, floodplains, vleis and other open areas, including open woodland. **Habits:** Diurnal; groups, called sounders, consist of an adult male, adult female and her offspring. Maternity and bachelor groups, and solitary individuals, are also found. **Food:** They are generally vegetarian. **Spoor:** Hooves are narrower than those of bushpigs (see opposite page); the dew claws usually mark clearly in the spoor. Defecates randomly, and is prone to rubbing itself against any convenient object. Often wallows in mud.

Warthog droppings

forefoot   hind foot

Bushpig

Potamochoerus porcus

Nigel Dennis/SIL

This animal's overall colour varies, but it is commonly reddish brown, with a dorsal crest of long, white hair. **Size:** Shoulder height 55–88 cm; mass 60–115 kg. **Habitat:** Bushpigs are predominantly nocturnal, with some daytime activity. Gregarious; they move in groups of from six to eight. **Food:** Omnivorous. **Spoor:** Hooves are broader than those of warthogs (see opposite page), and the dew claws usually mark clearly in the spoor. Consistently uses the same routes to feeding areas, thereby forming narrow, clearly marked paths. Practises tree-marking by tusking; defecates in latrines.

Louis Liebenberg

0

8 cm

forefoot

0

7.5 cm

hind foot

101

Antbear (Aardvark)   *Orycteropus afer*

This unusual mammal has a humped back, long pig-like snout, long donkey-like ears and a thick, tapering tail. **Size:** Length 1.4–1.8 m; mass 40–70 kg. **Habitat:** Wide tolerance. **Habits:** It is almost exclusively nocturnal; generally solitary, although one sees pairs (at mating time) and females with young. **Food:** Mainly termites in summer, ants in winter. **Spoor:** Four toes on the forefeet, five on the hind. The toes are armed with stout, broad claws. The front footprints show three toes and their claws: the first toe is absent, and only the tip of the fifth claw marks in the spoor. The hind footprint shows the three middle toes and claws, and only the tips of the first and fifth claws mark in the spoor. The hind footprints usually lie close behind or slightly overlying the front ones. Apart from small exploratory scratchings, the antbear makes three types of excavations: shallow diggings to gain access to food; shallow, temporary refuges that may run several metres underground; and a much more permanent structure used as a shelter in which the young are born. These shelters often have an extensive burrow system with several entrances. Unoccupied burrows provide shelter and safe refuge for a wide variety of mammals, birds, reptiles and insects. The antbear buries its faeces and does not use latrines; the droppings are ovoid and consist mainly of sand and other indigestible matter.

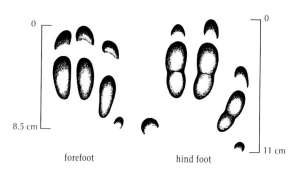

forefoot   hind foot

Blue Duiker   *Philantomba monticola*

HPH Photography/Photo Access

Southern Africa's smallest antelope, distinguished by its large eyes and slim legs. Colour of the upperparts varies: it can be a dark smokey brown with a dark bluish sheen, rusty brown, or dark brown. Both sexes carry tiny horns. **Size:** Shoulder height 35 cm; mass 4 kg. **Habitat:** Confined to forests, thickets and dense coastal bush. **Habits:** The animal is usually solitary; active in the early morning and after sunset. **Food:** A browser (eats freshly fallen forest-floor leaves). **Spoor:** The blue duiker creates well-marked paths on its routes between its resting, feeding and drinking places.

Louis Liebenberg

0

2.5 cm

forefoot

0

2.3 cm

hind foot

Red Duiker

Cephalophus natalensis

Roger de la Harpe/SIL

This attractive little antelope has chestnut red or orange-red upperparts. Both sexes carry the short, straight horns. **Size:** Shoulder height 43 cm; mass up to 14 kg. **Habitat:** Associated with forest and dense thicket near water. **Habits:** Solitary, or female with offspring. Mainly active at night. **Food:** The species is a browser. **Spoor:** Red duikers use communal dung heaps.

Louis Liebenberg

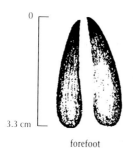

0   0

3.3 cm   3.5 cm

forefoot   hind foot

Common Duiker *Sylvicapra grimmia*

Nigel Dennis/SIL

This smallish antelope, whose colour varies from a grizzled grey to a yellowish-fawn, has a characteristic black band running from nose to forehead. Only the males carry horns, which are short and straight. **Size:** Shoulder height 50 cm; mass 18–21 kg. **Habitat:** Needs bush for shelter, shade and food. Wide tolerance; has a preference for savanna woodland. **Habits:** Solitary; found in pairs when females are in oestrus; also female with single young. Mainly active in the early morning, and late afternoon – extending well into the night. **Food:** Almost exclusively a browser. **Spoor:** Uses secretions from its facial glands to mark its territory. Droppings are round and pellet-like.

Louis Liebenberg

Pellet-like droppings

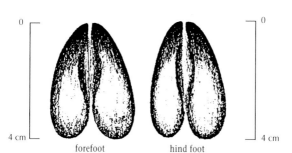

forefoot   hind foot

Suni

Neotragus moschatus

Clem Haagner/Gallo Images

The suni's upperparts are rufous-brown with a slightly speckled appearance, and the underparts are white. Only the males carry horns. **Size:** Shoulder height 35 cm; mass 5 kg. **Habitat:** Found in dry woodland, with thickets and underbrush. **Habits:** Usually solitary, but may be found in pairs or in family groups. Suni are mainly active in the early morning and late afternoon. **Food:** The animal is a browser. **Spoor:** The Suni uses communal latrines. It also demarcates its territory with secretions from facial glands.

forefoot   hind foot

Damara Dik-dik

Madoqua kirkii

Nigel Dennis/SIL

The upperparts of this attractive little animal are yellowish grey; only the males carry the small, straight horns. The nose is elongated, mobile, proboscis-like. **Size:** Shoulder height 38 cm; mass 5 kg. **Habitat:** Dense woodland and thicket on stony or hard clay ground. **Habits:** Occurs singly, in pairs or in family groups. Active at sunrise, in the late afternoon and at dusk, with some activity after dark. **Food:** Predominantly a browser. **Spoor:** The animal uses communal dung heaps; a male will paw the old dung into a heap with the forefeet, urinate on it and may paw again before defecating. Afterwards it wipes its preorbital glands on the nearest grass stems or scrubs.

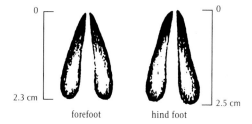

0   0

2.3 cm   2.5 cm

forefoot   hind foot

Sharpe's Grysbok

Raphicerus sharpei

Nigel Dennis

This antelope's body is a rich reddish brown, sprinkled with white hairs. Only the males carry the short horns. **Size:** Shoulder height 50 cm; mass 7.5 kg. **Habitat:** Found in areas of low-growing scrub and grass of medium height. **Habits:** Usually occurs singly, in pairs, or female with single offspring. Mainly nocturnal, but also active in the early morning and late afternoon. **Food:** Predominantly a browser. **Spoor:** Often returns to the same place to deposit droppings, which form heaps.

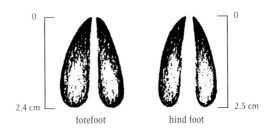

0   0

2.4 cm   2.5 cm

forefoot   hind foot

Grysbok

Raphicerus melanotis

Nigel Dennis

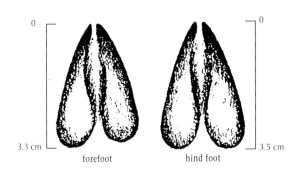

The grysbok's upperparts are rufous-brown sprinkled with white hairs, giving it a grizzled appearance. Only the males have horns. **Size:** Shoulder height 54 cm; mass 10 kg. **Habitat:** Thick scrub bush. **Habits:** Nocturnal; they are mainly solitary; females with young, or pairs are found, during the mating period. **Food:** Predominantly a grazer. **Spoor:** The grysbok deposits its droppings in dung heaps.

0	0
3.3 cm	3.5 cm
forefoot	hind foot

Steenbok

Raphicerus campestris

The upperparts of the steenbok are reddish brown, the underparts white. Ears very large; only the males carry horns. **Size:** Shoulder height 50 cm; mass 11 kg. **Habitat:** Associated with open grassland with some cover; also found in open woodland. **Habits:** Solitary, except when the male is attending female in oestrus, or female is still with her young. Mainly diurnal; active in the early morning and late evening.

Food: Both browse and graze.

Spoor: The animal's latrines tend to be situated near the perimeter of its territory. When defecating or urinating it will clear a spot with the front hooves, defecate or urinate, and then cover up the faeces by scraping soil over them with its front feet.

Steenbok droppings

forefoot
4 cm
0

hind foot
4.2 cm
0

Oribi

Ourebia ourebi

HPH Photography/Photo Access

The colour of the oribi's upperparts is yellowish rufous, the underparts white; tail black and bushy on the upper surface; the neck longer and thinner than that of the steenbok (see opposite page). Only the males have horns. **Size:** Shoulder height 60 cm; mass 14 kg. **Habitat:** Prefers open country, such as open grassland or floodplains. **Habits:** Found solitary, in pairs, or in parties comprising male and either one or two females with their offspring. **Food:** Predominantly a grazer, but will also browse. **Spoor:** Uses communal dung heaps. Marks grass stems with preorbital glands, leaving a small amount of black secretion.

Louis Liebenberg

Oribi droppings

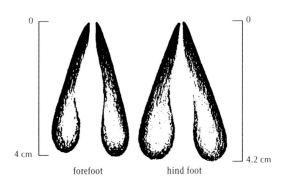

forefoot   hind foot

Klipspringer *Oreotragus oreotragus*

Peter Pickford/SIL

The colour of this agile antelope varies from speckled, yellowish brown to greyish brown; the coat has a coarse texture that blends in with the rocks among which it lives. Only the males carry horns. **Size:** Shoulder height 60 cm; mass 10–13 kg. **Habitat:** Restricted to a rocky habitat. **Habits:** Found in pairs, singly, or in small family groups. Browses or grazes on the flatter ground surrounding its habitat, but if disturbed will run for rocky shelter. Active in the early morning and late afternoon. **Food:** Predominantly a browser. **Spoor:** Walks on the tips of its hooves, which have long, narrow soles and blunt, rounded tips. The rounded hooves are an adaptation to the rocky terrain it inhabits. Other signs: Scent-marks by smearing a black, tarry secretion from its preorbital glands onto twigs. Scatters dung heaps throughout its territory; tends to defecate on or near the territorial border.

forefoot   hind foot

Springbok   *Antidorcas marsupialis*

Jean du Plessis

 This medium-sized antelope's back is a bright cinnamon-brown with a broad, dark reddish brown horizontal band separating the upperparts from the white underparts. Both sexes carry horns. The common name is derived from the way the animal springs or bounds with its back arched to expose a white ridge of hair, a display known as 'pronking' and said to advertise its fitness to other springbok and to predators. **Size:** Shoulder height 75 cm; mass 37–41 kg. **Habitat:** The animal is associated with the arid regions and open grassland. **Habits:** Gregarious. Active in the early morning and late afternoon; some activity after dark. **Food:** Both browse and graze. **Spoor:** Marks its territory with conspicuous latrines.

Louis Liebenberg

0   0

forefoot   hind foot

5.5 cm   5.8 cm

Impala

Aepyceros melampus

The upperparts of this graceful, medium-sized antelope are a rich reddish brown, the flanks reddish pale fawn, the underparts white. Only the males carry horns. Hind legs have black glands just above the hoof, called metatarsals, which are diagnostic. **Size:** Shoulder height 90 cm; mass from 40–50 kg. **Habitat:** Associated with woodland. **Habits:** Gregarious. **Food:** Both browse and graze. **Spoor:** The male creates dung heaps during the rut (mating season), which are scattered within the territory. At other times both sexes urinate and defecate at random.

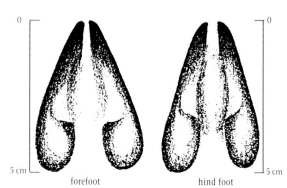

0   0

5 cm   5 cm

forefoot   hind foot

Grey Rhebok

Pelea capreolus

Nigel Dennis/SIL

The grey rhebok has a long, slender neck and long, narrow pointed ears. The upperparts of its body and flanks are greyish brown, the underparts white; the hair short, thick and woolly. Only the males of the species carry horns.
Size: Shoulder height 75 cm; mass 20 kg. **Habitat:** Associated with rocky hills, rocky mountain slopes and mountain plateaux with good grass cover. **Habits:** Solitary males, and family parties numbering up to 12 individuals can be seen. Active throughout the day. **Food:** Grass. **Spoor:** Similar to that of mountain reedbuck (see page 116) but slightly narrower and sharper.

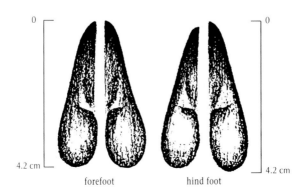

forefoot   hind foot

Mountain Reedbuck
Redunca fulvorufula

Anup Shah/Gallo Images

This medium-sized antelope's overall colour is greyish on the upperparts, the neck reddish, the underparts white. Its coat is soft and woolly, its tail bushy. The characteristic gland located just below the ears appears as a black patch. Only the males carry the short, heavily ridged, forward-pointing horns.

Size: Shoulder height 72 cm; mass 30 kg. **Habitat:** The dry, grass-covered, stony slopes of hills and mountains where there is cover in the way of bushes or scattered trees. **Habits:** Usually occurs in small groups of three to six, but also in herds of up to 30. The animal is at its most active in the early mornings, late afternoons and at night. **Food:** The mountain reedbuck is almost exclusively a grazer. **Spoor:** This is similar to that of the grey rhebok (see page 115) but slightly broader.

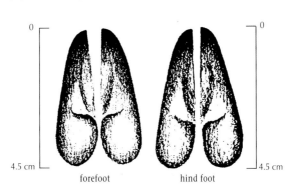

| 0 | 0 |

4.5 cm   4.5 cm

forefoot   hind foot

Reedbuck

Redunca arundinum

Lex Hes

The reedbuck's overall body colour varies from brown, tending to grey or buffy grey, yellow or buffy yellow or greyish brown. The back is usually slightly darker; the underparts are white. Only the males carry horns. **Size:** Shoulder height 80–95 cm; mass 50–70 kg. **Habitat:** Essential habitat requirements include cover, in the form of tall grass or reedbeds, and a good water supply; the animal is usually found in vleis with a wet drainage area or grassland adjacent to streams, rivers or other areas of permanent water. **Habits:** Lives in pairs or family parties. **Food:** Almost exclusively a grazer. **Spoor:** Tends to use fixed trails leading to water. Before lying down, it will trample the ground, breaking down the grass to form a bed.

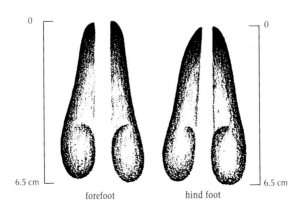

0   0

6.5 cm   6.5 cm

forefoot   hind foot

Red Lechwe

Kobus leche

The upperparts of this antelope's body and flanks are reddish yellow, the underparts white, the lower legs black. Only the males carry horns. **Size:** Shoulder height 1 m; mass 100 kg. **Habitat:** A water-loving species found in the shallow inundations of floodplain fringing swamps and rivers; and in high-standing beds of papyrus, reeds and semi-aquatic grasses on the fringes of dry land. **Habits:** Gregarious; found in small herds of 15–20 individuals. Active before sunrise and in the early morning, and again in the late afternoon and, for a time, after sunset. **Food:** Almost exclusively a grazer. **Spoor:** The hooves of the lechwe are distinctly elongated, although not so much as those of the sitatunga (see page 121). They splay sideways on soft ground, which helps the animal to negotiate muddy terrain.

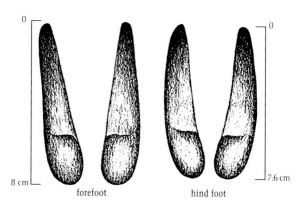

forefoot hind foot

Puku

Kobus vardonii

 Sometimes confused with the impala (see page 114), but the puku's horns do not spiral. The upperparts of the puku's body are golden yellow, the underparts lighter. Restricted to a narrow stretch on the Caprivi region of Namibia; found nowhere else in southern Africa. Only the males carry horns. **Size:** Shoulder height 80 cm; mass 62–74 kg. **Habitat:** The puku is associated with grassy areas in the immediate vicinity of water. **Habits:** Gregarious; crepuscular. **Food:** Predominantly a grazer. **Spoor:** Elongated hoofs, adapted for soft, muddy ground.

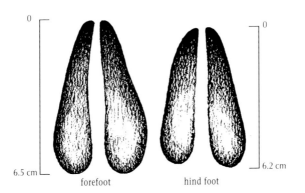

0	0
forefoot	hind foot
6.5 cm	6.2 cm

Waterbuck

Kobus ellipsiprymnus

Nigel Dennis/SIL

The colour of this large antelope's upperparts is variable: it may be a dark brownish grey or greyish brown, grizzled with white and grey hairs. A characteristic white ring encircles the rump. Only the males carry horns. **Size:** Shoulder height 1.3 m; mass 250–270 kg. **Habitat:** Associated with water. **Habits:** Gregarious; active during all but the hottest hours of the day. **Food:** Predominantly a grazer, but also browses. **Spoor:** Roughly triangular-shaped hoofprints, which are quite characteristic.

Louis Liebenberg

| forefoot | hind foot |

0 ⌐ ... ⌐ 0
9 cm ⌐ ... ⌐ 8.5 cm

Sitatunga

Tragelaphus spekei

Chris & Tilde Stuart

Adult males are dark drab brown (females similar, or redder). The hair is long, coarse and shaggy. Only males carry horns. **Size:** Shoulder height 90 cm; mass 115 kg. **Habitat:** Usually found in dense papyrus and reedbeds in swamp areas, in water up to a metre deep; sometimes feeds in woodland fringes. **Habits:** Semi-aquatic; active most of the day, except during the hottest hours. Occurs in small herds of up to about six individuals. An excellent swimmer. **Food:** Aquatic grasses, plants growing in the shallower water, and the freshly sprouting tips of reeds. **Spoor:** The adult male sitatunga's elongated, widely splayed hooves may reach a length of up to 18 cm on the forefeet and up to 16 cm on the hind (the measurements given below are those actually recorded by the author). Uses established paths when moving from a swamp to woodland.

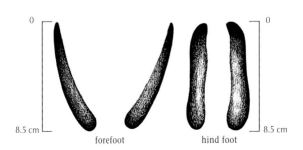

0			0
8.5 cm			8.5 cm
	forefoot	hind foot	

Bushbuck   *Tragelaphus scriptus*

Lex Hes

 Individual bushbuck vary widely in size over their range. Their general colour also varies, from chestnut to dark brown. All the animals, however, have a conspicuous white collar, with white spots on cheeks and flanks; flanks and hind quarters sometimes show stripes. Only the males carry horns.
Size: The average shoulder height is 80 cm; mass 45 kg.
Habitat: Closely associated with riverine or other types of underbrush close to permanent water supplies. **Habits:** Generally solitary; also occurs in small groups of two or three. Active at night, in early morning and late evening. **Food:** Mainly a browser, but also grazes. **Spoor:** Heart-shaped hoof, similar to that of common duiker (see page 105) but larger.

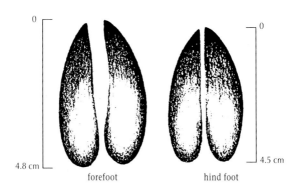

0   0

4.8 cm   4.5 cm

forefoot   hind foot

Kudu

Tragelaphus strepsiceros

 A large fawn-grey antelope with 6–10 vertical white stripes on the sides. Usually, only the males carry horns, which are long and deeply spiralled. **Size:** Shoulder height 140–155 cm; mass 180–250 kg. **Habitat:** Savanna woodland. **Habits:** Gregarious; occurs in small herds, usually up to four or so individuals. Adult males may be solitary. Most active in the early morning and late afternoon. **Food:** A browser. **Spoor:** The male's forefoot is proportionately broader than that of the female.

Nyala

Tragelaphus angasii

Peter Pickford/SIL

A largish antelope, the sexes markedly different in appearance. The male has a shaggy, greyish coat with a white crest on the back and long hair on the neck, belly and rump, and 9–14 vertical white stripes down its sides. The female also carries the stripes but is much smaller, yellowish brown to chestnut in colour, and lacks the shaggy hair. Only the males carry horns. **Size:** Shoulder height 1.15 m; mass 62–108 kg. **Habitat:** Prefers thickets in dry savanna woodland, riverine woodland with thickets, and dry forest. **Habits:** Gregarious; occurs in groups of usually two or three individuals, but herds can number up to 30. Solitary males are also common. Both diurnal and nocturnal. **Food:** Predominantly a browser. **Spoor:** The forefoot of the male is larger and proportionately broader than that of the female.

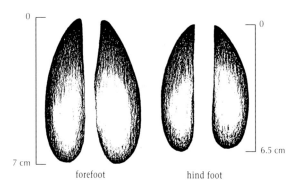

forefoot   hind foot

Eland

Taurotragus oryx

Nigel Dennis/SIL

The largest of Africa's antelopes, a light rufous-fawn in colour, with narrow white stripes down the flanks. Both sexes carry horns; the male's are much heavier than the female's. **Size:** Shoulder height 1.7 m; mass 450–700 kg. **Habitat:** Shows wide tolerance. **Habits:** Occurs in small herds, but occasionally in huge aggregations of more than 1,000. Active in mornings and afternoons. **Food:** Mainly a browser, but grazes fresh, sprouting grass after fire. **Spoor:** The hind foot is more elongated than that of the buffalo (see page 126) and of domestic cattle.

Louis Liebenberg

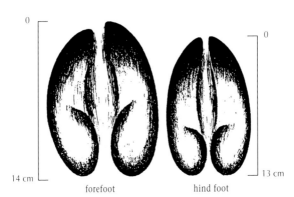

| forefoot | hind foot |

Buffalo

Syncerus caffer

Nigel Dennis/SIL

A massive animal, ox-like in general appearance. Old males are black; females show a tinge of reddish brown. The curved horns are huge in old adult males; those of the females are lighter. **Size:** Shoulder height 1.4 m; mass 550–700 kg.

Habitat: The buffalo prefers open woodland savanna and needs a plentiful supply of grass, shade and water. **Habits:** Gregarious; occurs in herds of up to several hundred. Most active in the evening, at night and in the morning. **Food:** Mainly a grazer, but also browses. **Spoor:** The dew claws, which show in soft mud, may not always mark on hard ground. The hind foot is not as elongated as that of the eland (see page 125).

Louis Liebenberg

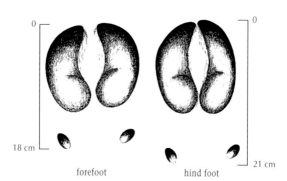

| 0 | | 0 |

18 cm

21 cm

forefoot   hind foot

Gemsbok
Oryx gazella

Nigel Dennis/SIL

A large antelope bearing conspicuous black markings on the body and face. The upperparts and flanks are a pale fawn-grey, underparts white, with a broad, dark-brown band in between. Horns are straight, rapier-like, the female's more slender than the male's. **Size:** Shoulder height 1.2 m; mass 210–240 kg. **Habitat:** Open, arid country. **Habits:** Gregarious; occurs in herds of up to 12, though solitary males are common. Active during early morning and late afternoon. **Food:** Mainly graze. **Spoor:** The gemsbok will dig in sand with its front hooves for water, and for succulent roots, rhizomes and bulbs. When defecating, territorial males adopt a characteristically low, crouching posture, which ensures that the faecal pellets lie in a small pile and so retain their odour longer. Before defecating, the animal will paw the ground, transferring secretions from the pedal glands to the earth. Males will also horn vegetation to mark their territory.

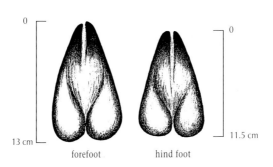

forefoot   hind foot

Sable Antelope

Hippotragus niger

Daryl Balfour

A large, handsome species, the old males of which are black, the females a very dark brown, both with white underparts. Both sexes carry horns, which are more slender in females. **Size:** Shoulder height 135 cm; mass 180–270 kg. **Habitat:** Savanna woodland. **Habits:** Gregarious, occurs in herds of 20–30 individuals. Bulls are often solitary. The animal is at its most active in the early morning and late afternoon. **Food:** Predominantly a grazer, but the animal will browse in some areas. **Spoor:** Territorial sable males break branches and strip bark with their horns, which may be a way of marking the territory.

Louis Liebenberg

0	0
9.5 cm	9 cm
forefoot	hind foot

Roan Antelope

Hippotragus equinus

Anton Pauw

 A large, greyish-brown antelope with a black face, a contrasting white patch around the nose and mouth and a white patch on each cheek. **Size:** Shoulder height 110–150 cm; mass 220–300 kg. **Habitat:** Confined to lightly wooded savanna with extensive open areas of medium to tall grasses and available water. **Habits:** Gregarious; occurs in small herds of 5–12 individuals, sometimes up to 25. Active from sunrise until mid-morning, and in the late afternoon. **Food:** Predominantly a grazer, but also browses. **Spoor:** *Hippotragus* antelope will horn bushes, grass, and the ground. They also establish their presence by defecating, urinating and scent-marking the area with their pedal glands.

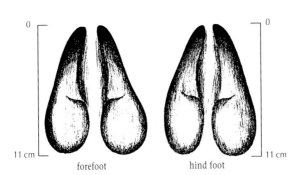

forefoot   hind foot

Bontebok

Damaliscus dorcas dorcas

A medium-sized antelope with a rich dark-brown body colour and a contrasting white rump patch, underparts and face blaze. The latter runs down between the eyes and, unlike that of the blesbok is not divided by a transverse brown band. The horns of the female are more slender than those of the male. **Size:** Shoulder height 90 cm; mass 62 kg. **Habitat:** Natural distribution restricted to one area in the southwestern Cape. **Habits:** Gregarious; diurnal, mainly active in the early morning and late afternoon. **Food:** The bontebok is almost exclusively a grazer. **Spoor:** The latrines of the territorial male are scattered around its territory and are generally disregarded by other males. A central latrine is often used as a resting place during the day.

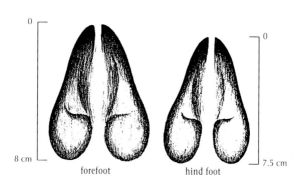

forefoot   hind foot

Blesbok   *Damaliscus dorcas phillipsi*

Nigel Dennis/SIL

A brown antelope with white underparts and a white face blaze divided just below the eyes by a narrow brown band. Both sexes carry horns. Unlike the bontebok it does not have a white rump-patch. **Size:** Shoulder height 95 cm; mass 70 kg. **Habitat:** Grassland, with sources of water. **Habits:** Gregarious; diurnal; active in the early morning and late evening. **Food:** Predominantly a grazer, but will occasionally browse. **Spoor:** When travelling to their feeding or drinking places, and when returning to their night resting sites, blesbok move in long, single files – a routine that creates distinct paths. The species marks its territory by inserting grass stems in its preorbital glands, or by wiping the glands across vegetation (to smear them with secretion). The territorial male leaves dung patches in its territory, and tends to lie on them during resting periods.

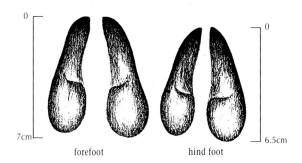

forefoot   hind foot

Tsessebe

Damaliscus lunatus

Peter Pickford/SIL

A largish antelope with a long, narrow face, shoulders that stand conspicuously higher than the rump, and a dark reddish brown body with a distinct purplish sheen. **Size:** Shoulder height 1.2 m; mass 126–140 kg. **Habitat:** Open savanna woodland close to grassland plains; needs water and shade.

Habits: Gregarious; Tsessebe are active mainly in the morning and evening. **Food:** Almost exclusively a grazer. **Spoor:** Both sexes mark with their preorbital glands, rub the sides of their faces on the ground, and horn the ground. Territorial males paw and scrape the surface to mark their territories.

Louis Liebenberg

forefoot

hind foot

Red Hartebeest *Alcelaphus buselaphus*

A medium-sized, high-shouldered animal, generally a reddish brown in colour but this varies according to the race and region and may be yellow-fawn or tawny. Both sexes carry horns, the male's heavier in build than those of the female. **Size:** Shoulder height 125 cm; mass 120–150 kg. **Habitat:** Associated with open country. **Habits:** Gregarious; at its most active in the early morning and the late afternoon. **Food:** Predominantly a grazer. **Spoor:** Hoof triangular in shape, similar to that of tsessebe (see opposite page).

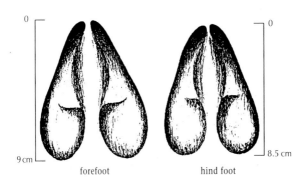

forefoot   hind foot

Black Wildebeest   *Connochaetes gnou*

This relative of the antelopes is generally buffy brown in colour and has a characteristic tail with long, white hair reaching to the ground. Both sexes carry horns. **Size:** Shoulder height 1.2 m; mass 100–180 kg. **Habitat:** Open plains, grasslands and Karoo country. **Habits:** Gregarious; active at dawn, in the early morning, late afternoon and after sunset. **Food:** Predominantly a grazer. **Spoor:** The animal scent-marks its territory with faeces and urine, and with its preorbital and interdigital glands. Territorial black wildebeest paw the ground vigorously before defecating.

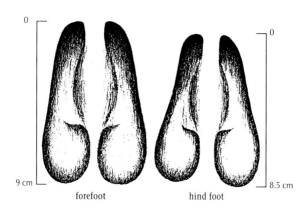

forefoot   hind foot

Blue Wildebeest

Connochaetes taurinus

Nigel Dennis/SIL

Similar in appearance to the black wildebeest (see opposite page) but dark grey in colour and with a mane of long black hair, and long, black hair at the end of its tail. Both sexes carry horns; the female's horns are lighter in build than those of the male. **Size:** Shoulder height 1.5 m; mass 250 kg. **Habitat:** Associated with savanna woodland and open grassland. **Habits:** Gregarious; active in the morning and afternoon. **Food:** The species is a grazer. **Spoor:** Territorial males mark their territories by dropping on to their knees and rubbing their preorbital glands on the ground, on bushes and on tree trunks.

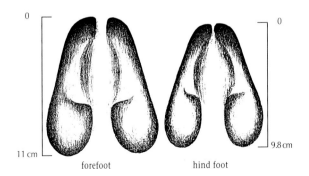

forefoot   hind foot

DROPPINGS: A SELECT CHECKLIST
Measurements refer to length

Hare, 1 cm

Dassie, 1 cm

Small antelope, 1 cm

Springhare,
2 cm

Medium antelope,
1–2 cm

Antbear, 4 cm

Giraffe, 2–3 cm

Warthog, 5 cm

Porcupine,
5 cm

Baboon, 5–10 cm

Zebra, 5 cm

Monkey, 3–5 cm

Small carnivore, 5 cm

Otter, 8 cm

Hyaena, 5 cm

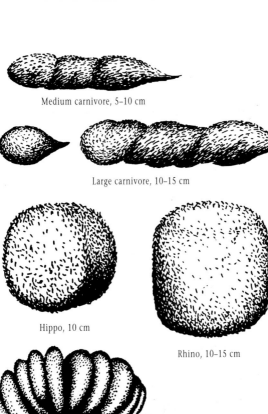

Medium carnivore, 5–10 cm

Large carnivore, 10–15 cm

Hippo, 10 cm

Rhino, 10–15 cm

Buffalo, 15 cm (widest part)

Elephant, 15–20 cm
(widest part)

GLOSSARY

Arboreal: Living in trees.
Carnivore: A flesh-eating animal
Crepuscular: Active at twlight and/or just before dawn.
Dew claw: The rudimentary first digit on the feet of canids.
Diagnostic: A distinctive feature characteristic of a species.
Diurnal: Active during the day.
Dorsal: Relating to the back or spine.
Gregarious: Living in groups (herds, colonies and so forth)
Habitat: The environment in which a plant or animal lives in its natural state.
Herbivore: An animal that feeds on grasses (a grazer), leaves (a browser) and other vegetable matter.
Insectivore: An animal that eats insects.
Interdigital (gland): Located between toes or hooves.
Latrine: The place where an animal, or a group of animals, deposits faeces.
Nocturnal: Active at night.
Ocelli: The simple, light-sensitive eyes of insects and some other invertebrates.
Oestrus: The period during which a female mammal is sexually receptive.
Pedal (gland): Located on the foot.
Preorbital (gland): Located in front of the eye-socket.
Protractile: Able to be extended or protruded.
Scats: Another word for droppings, usually those of certain small mammals.
Spoor: The trail of an animal, notably its tracks but also other signs of its passage.
Substrate: Underlying layer; the inorganic material on which a plant grows or an animal moves.
Termitaria: The nests of a termite colony.
Terrestrial: Living at ground level.
Territory: A limited area occupied, and defended, by an animal.
Ventral: Relating to the front part of the body; towards the belly.

FOOTPRINT TERMS

claws
toes
intermediate pads
proximal pads

FURTHER READING

Liebenberg, L. 1990. *A Field Guide to the Animal Tracks of Southern Africa.* David Philip Publishers, Cape Town.

Liebenberg, L. 1990. *The Art of Tracking: The Origin of Science* David Philip Publishers, Cape Town.

MacLean, G. l. 1993. *Roberts' Birds of Southern Africa.* The Trustees of the John Voelcker Bird Book Fund, Cape Town.

Newman, K.B. 1993 (6th edition, first impression 1998). *Newman's Birds of Southern Africa.* Southern Book Publishers, Johannesburg.

Stuart, C. and Stuart, T. 1994. *A Field Guide to the Tracks & Signs of Southern and East African Wildlife.* Southern Book Publishers, Johannesburg.

Stuart, C. and Stuart, T. 1992. *Field Guide to the Mammals of Southern Africa.* Struik Publishers, Cape Town.

INTERNET INFORMATION

Authors site: www.cybertracker.co.za

INDEX

Struik Publishers
(a division of New Holland Publishing (South Africa) (Pty) Ltd)
Cornelis Struik House
80 McKenzie Street
Cape Town 8001

New Holland Publishing is a
member of the Johnnic Publishing Group.
www.struik.co.za
Log on to our photographic website
www.imagesofafrica.co.za for an African experience.

First published 2000
10 9 8 7 6 5 4 3 2

Publishing manager: Pippa Parker
Managing editor: Simon Pooley
Editor: Peter Joyce
Designer: Dominic Robson
Proofreader: Brenda Brickman

Reproduction by Hirt and Carter Cape (Pty) Ltd
Printed and bound by Times Offset (M) Sdn Bhd, Malaysia

ISBN 1 86872 008 X

Front cover: Sidewinder (Anthony Bannister/ABPL)
Back cover: Burchell's zebra (Nigel Dennis/SIL)
Title page: Black-backed jackal (Nigel Dennis/SIL)